Business Breakthrough Prayers

Overcoming Business Challenges

BUSINESS BREAKTHROUGH PRAYERS
Copyright © 2017 by Olatunde Oluwabunmi Judah

ISBN: 978-1533013927

Printed by CreateSpace, An Amazon.com Company

All correspondence to:
Olatunde Oluwabunmi Judah
Divine Storm Assembly Ministries
20, Oluwole Olaniyan Street,
Iyana Ipaja.
Lagos Nigeria
Mobile: 2348067719589, E-mail: dsachurch@gmail.com

Published by: Goshen Publishing House, Lagos, Nigeria.
And Divine Storm Assembly, Worldwide
Mobile: 2348067719589

Available at Amazon.com, other online stores and book stores.

ACKNOWLEDGEMENT

I am sending out my sincere appreciation to the fathers God has brought my way who has thought me the secrets of prayers and who has also given me the platform to demonstrate the potency of prayers in life and ministry.

I sincerely appreciate Pastor Wole Oladiyun of Christ Living Spring Apostolic Ministry (CLAM), you exposed me and many to the deliverance and victory behind warfare prayers and the joy of the freedom in praying through. Thank you for making us pray through into breakthrough.

I appreciate Pastor Peace and Pastor Mrs Funmilayo Akingunsoye of Calvary freedom Apostolic Ministry (Cafam), for been a father to look up to. God bless you.

I appreciate Pastor Joshua Idikwu and Deaconess Agnes Idikwu of Faithful Family Foundation, for your all time believes in me and unwavering support and fatherly love. You are a blessing may the Lord keep you in Jesus name.

I appreciate my friend and my partner in life, Oluwaseun Damilohun for being a gift from God, a blessing, a joy giver. May God keep us.

I appreciate all my friends, all workers of DSA, and loved ones. Thank you for encouraging and supporting me. May the Lord bless you all.

CONTENTS

Section 4: Prayer For The Business Man

Dedication

I dedicate this book to God almighty, who inspires this book idea at solution night, in CLAM. 2014. And there was unusual grace released to make it easy for me to write. To God be the glory.

INTRODUCTION

God is interested in the success of your business because it is God that inspires business idea in men to bring them wealth and make their life meaningful. God wants to see you succeed as much as you desire to succeed in your endeavors. However, some business cannot attain their dream except some spiritual measure is put in place.

Jesus spoke this parable.
He said therefore, A certain nobleman went into a far country to receive for himself a kingdom, and to return. And he called his ten servants, and delivered them ten pounds, and said unto them, Occupy till I come. Luke 19:13.

The man in question is like God giving the children of men idea to implement and be a blessing to their generation. He said occupy till I come. God wants you to occupy space on earth with your idea, to touch lives, to help people to make a living through your business.

Many people are given to do business. Some were created for the sole purpose of becoming an employer of labor. So before they were born, there is been a business seed in them. That is the like of the pounds he gave them. But when the time comes for them to manifest the seed, they will begin to have a desire to do a business, in the process, their zeal will arouse, they will ask question like what can I do, and God will impress in them the business idea he has dropped in them.

The spirit of man [is] the candle of the LORD, searching all the inward parts of the belly. Prov. 20:27

Every man has this candle in them, it is the search light for the deposit of idea God put in men. It is crucial to understand that any carrier of a seed is a planter. He plants his seed to create his harvest. The more he realizes he needs more harvest, and then he will have to plant more seeds to create more harvest.

Likewise, whatever is yielding you money in one way or the other is a business. Business is a door to wealth, people, and opportunities.

God has given you that business to bless you and to make you a blessing to others. That is why he will release all the resources needed for you to excel in the business.

There was a man called Peter, Luke 5: 1-7. Peter was a business man. He is in the business of sea foods called fishing. He went out this day and labored all night, and he caught no fish, but when He encountered Jesus, the initiator of Business. He commanded him to cast his net into the sea again. But Peter said to him, I have done what you are telling me several times, before you came here but I caught nothing, but at your word…and he tried again. And there was a breakthrough; in so much that his boat could not contain it, for the harvest was so great.

Truths
1. It is God that prospers business.
2. God answers the prayer of business men.
3. Business breakthrough is your birthright.
4. It is God that can guide a business to success.
5. God is ready to help you succeed.
6. There is nothing difficult with God.

It is Christ that holds the key of business breakthrough in his hand, and he is ready to give it to you now. He said to the same Peter, I will give unto you the keys of the kingdom of heaven, that when you open no man can shut, when you shut no man can open. Matt. 16:18.

Come to him through his word, and discover the keys you need to turn your business around; however, prayer is one of the keys. He said, Open your mouth wide and I will fill it. Ps. 81:10 It's only what you pray for you are permitted to receive. When you go to a shopping mart to buy anything, it is what you pay for they will give you. What you don't pray for don't expect.
God is moved by the prayer of his children. Either you pray or sow a seed as you are led by God. That is great keys that break fallow ground in business. As you read on, pray all this prayers with faith and understanding.

Every wrong circumstance in business can be corrected through the right prayers. Prayers are given to change the situation of men and things. It is your turn to have a change of story as you pray these prophetic prayers.

God led Isaac to Gerar and he promised to bless him, and he did blessed him. Then Isaac sowed in that land, and received in the same year an hundredfold: and the LORD blessed him. And the man waxed great, and went forward, and grew until he became very great: For he had possession of flocks, and possession of herds, and great store of servants: and the Philistines envied him. Genesis 26:1-12,

This book is not a business experimental formula. Any formula designed by men can work and fail. It can work for one business and never work for the other. But this is a scriptural formula, which cannot fail. He upholds all things by the word of his power, and the earth has never failed. The right application of the scripture is the only formula that will bring practical solution to any problem without fail, *job said…Acquaint now thyself with him, and be at peace: thereby good shall come unto thee. Receive, I pray thee, the law from his mouth, and lay up his words in thine heart. If thou return to the Almighty, thou shalt be built up, thou shalt put away iniquity far from thy tabernacles. Then shalt thou layup gold as dust, and the [gold] of Ophir as the stones of the brooks. Yea, the Almighty shall be thy defence, and thou shalt have plenty of silver.*
When [men] are cast down, then thou shalt say, [There is] lifting up; and he shall save the humble person. Job 22:21-25, 29

HOW IT IS RIGHTLY APPLIED

By Revelational Understanding
Revelation means to have access to hidden secrets, to see outstanding part of a standing thing. Revelation is when your spiritual eyes is opened and depth of understanding deepens by

the knowledge exposed to you. When you engage the word to a problem, it delivers the result expected of it.

You have to come to the agreement of God's instruction through his word, and believe in it, before you apply it. The word answers to those who agree with it, since he is a personality.

Every word of God has a problem it is designed to solve. The word is a spiritual formula for the challenges of life and business.

By Faith

Now faith is the substance of things hoped for, the evidence of things not seen. For by it the elders obtained a good report. Heb 11:1-2

Faith is a raw material for change. Until faith is engaged, result cannot be realized. Faith is a spiritual converter. It converts your expectation to a tangible substance.

The law of faith works for those who believe in it and the evidence of your believe is your action.

Your faith is your thermometer to regulate the heat of the business. With your faith in place, you control the situation of the business and you determine the success of the business. Faith keeps you in control of the business.

By Authority

Authority is the standing power of God in your mouth. It takes divine authority to give divine command. Authority makes you bold and courageous. There is authority inside of you through the deposit of power God has placed in you.

Death and life [are] in the power of the tongue: and they that love it shall eat the fruit thereof. Prov. 18:21

There is power of life and death in the tongue. And you will eat the fruit of it. There is innate authority for being the son of God in you. Authority is activated by faith. Every son of a king has some measure of authority. You are the son of the King of kings. You will not know what you are able to do, until you decree a thing and God establishes it.

By Declaration

Thou shalt also decree a thing, and it shall be established unto thee: and the light shall shine upon thy ways. Job 22:28

Declaration means to say something loudly and openly, to confess and decree a thing. He said you shall say to this mountain. To say is to declare. He said, you shall decree a thing and it shall be established, and light will shine upon your path. To decree is to issue out utterance into a situation for a turn around. Whatever you decree shall be established.

By The Name Of Jesus

And whatsoever ye shall ask in my name, that will I do, that the Father may be glorified in the Son. ye shall ask any thing in my name, I will do [it]. John 14:13-14

That name is above every problem, it is above that storm, it is above that challenge, that situation and debt that business is in. Call it meltdown, debts, name it, the name of Jesus is above it. It is a name God has ordained to subdued other names. At the name every knee shall bow and every tongue shall confess that Jesus Christ is Lord to the glory of God the father.

That name will become a rod of authority in your hand to confront every physical and spiritual problem you are having in that business/organization.

It's the only name that everything in creation obeys. It's the only name that carries the power to turn things around. It's the only name that opens doors physically and spiritually. It's the only name that can bail you out. It's the only name that is given men to save. It's the only name that God recognizes; even the devil hears it and tremble. It's the only name that when it is engaged the person behind the name is at work to honor his name at anytime, anywhere and any situation. It's the only name that never changes. Engage the name of Jesus.

Section 1
Foundation For Business Success

CHAPTER 1

FOUNDATION FOR BUSINESS SUCCESS

...observe to do according to all that is written therein: for then thou shalt make thy way prosperous, and then thou shalt have good success. Josh. 1:8

Every flourishing business requires the right foundation to thrive. The foundation is what determines the formation for growth and progress in the business. Good foundation stands as a pillar for a business success. No success without a structure, and no structure without a solid foundation. Success in business is not a function of coincidence; it is a function of the foundation backing the business. Every true success story has a root in a standing and solid foundation. The founders determine the foundation. The speed of business success is also determined by the solidity of the foundation the business was laid upon. The deeper the root the taller the tree, the wider the roots the firmer the stem, the better the foundation the better the business will be.

Why?

Everything has a foundation. Good foundation is one of the secret many don't know as the major contributor to the success of any business. It takes the foundation to predict the possible outcome of the business. When the foundation of the business is right, expect success at the short or long run in the business. Foundation is the root, the source, the origin of the business. Right foundation is everything to the success of any venture in

15

life. The foundation here talks about how the business is been laid, the measures that were put in place to keep it running. If it is thriving, the foundation contributed to it, if it is not thriving, the foundation also contributed to it. If you get the foundation right, there is a possibility that the business will survive every storm that comes her way. This goes for every organization too

As to business, a faulty foundation will give birth to a faulty business. A strong foundation will give birth to a firm business, while a weak foundation will give birth to a weak business. You must pay maximum attention to the foundation you lay for the business, because that is where the success begins.

If the foundation is destroyed what can the righteous do? Ps. 11:3. If the foundation has a problem from the beginning, there will be a lot of problem in the going that will require coming back to the foundation to make correction before things can begin to work right.

In righteousness shalt thou be established: thou shalt be far from oppression; for thou shalt not fear: and from terror; for it shall not come near thee. Isa 54:14

When you start on a foundation laid by God's standard, your business will be far from oppression (challenges that will see you calling for men's help), far from (the fear of loses) no terror will come near (terror is the common physical and spiritual challenges business may have). God will be there to secure the business, because of it foundation. Every business and organization must sort for the foundation laid on standard of

God's word. Both small scale business and large scale business need a godly and right foundation.

Every lasting foundation is based on the word of God. All things were made by the word of God, without the word was not anything made that was made. So when a business is structured on the foundation of truth it will forever be growing and glowing in good times and bad times as well.

WHAT MAKES UP THE RIGHT FOUNDATION

A faulty foundation takes time to be repaired, while building a right foundation at the start is easy. This is the foundation of every successful business.

1. RIGHT INSPIRATION

But [there is] a spirit in man: and the inspiration of the Almighty giveth them understanding. Job 32:8

Every business today was once an idea in the heart of someone before it is given birth to. Divine inspiration is a channel of receiving ideas for what to do in life. It is God that reveals the idea of a business and impress the business strongly in you. Often times, the idea will go in line with what your senses approves and what you are comfortable with. There is the right business idea for anyone that God has raised to prosper in the area of business and industries. God does nothing by mistake, He's perfect in all his works. Every good idea however is product of divine inspiration. Look at sports stars and entertainment stars. God told Jeremiah, saying before I formed you, I have ordained you to be a prophet. It is not what God decided when they gave birth to Jeremiah; it has been ordained before he was formed in his mother's womb. However, every idea birthed by divine inspiration was pre ordained for you before you were born, but released into your heart when you were ripe to bring it forth and turn it into something great.

The Spirit of God works in line with the spirit of man, and so it release inspiration to the spirit of man. Every right business idea you received through inspiration is what you were born to do.

Divine inspiration can also come as a result of God revealing the business idea to you or impressing it strongly in your heart. If you are trusting God for a business idea, ask God to open your eyes and open your heart, if he does not drop it into your heart, he will show it to your eyes as an opportunity lying around you to grab and work with it.

2. RIGHT VISION

Getting a perfect business inspiration is wonderful, but having a perfect vision to match it up is the key that turns things on. Pairing your idea with vision is a wise thing to do. Through wisdom a house is built...Prov. 24:4. Vision is the direct picture of what you want your business to look like in the nearest future. Vision is painting the picture of the future of the business. Vision is like the wisdom that a business needs to succeed. The vision will help a lay man to catch the pathway that has been set for the business to prosper. Vision gives direction and guides the people that will carry out the ideas on what next, where next and how next. Vision gives the idea a breathing ground to thrive and succeed. You need to attach the

18

right vision to your God given business idea. Write down your vision and put it to work.

3. RIGHT BUSINESS NAME

Every business is like a child, the moment you give birth to them, you must be inspired by the right spirit to give it the right name. Whatever is not inspired by the spirit may not generate the expected impact needed to bring changes. Business is given by God for a purpose. God gives you business to be a blessing to mankind.

Everything God created has a name, inspired by the Spirit but given by man. God told Adam to name all the animals, and the name he gave them is what they were called till date. God inspires him to give them names. If you could observe, each names is perfect on each animal so well. The name of lion goes well with the creature called lion, likewise Elephant, man has not thought of changing any animal's name, because that was the perfect name for them. The name makes the brand a quality one.

So every divinely inspired business idea must have a suitable business name. Name is an identity that brings out the glory and fame of something. It announces a venture, and it also reflects the future of that venture.

And Abram fell on his face: and God talked with him, saying, *As for me, behold, my covenant [is] with thee, and thou shalt be a father of many nations. Neither shall thy name any more be called Abram, but thy name shall be Abraham; for a father of many nations have I made thee.*
Genesis 17:3-5

19

Look at some business names. For example, barns and nobles, google, facebook, those names sound perfect. They were inspired names. Sometimes the name may not be given directly by you, someone around you can suggest a name and your spirit will connect and agree with the genius of the name.

Whatever you take your time to do, you will get the best out of it. Take your time to decide a name for your business. When God inspired the name of the Holy Book, 'Bible', it sounds beautiful and perfect for it. That is the highest selling book till tomorrow. One generation to another will keep buying it.

So be inspired for the write name as well. If possible, pray that the spirit of God should reveal to you the name the business should be crested. When Elizabeth conceived, the Angel appeared to her and told her to call his name John. So John's name was revealed before he was born.

There is power in names. All this help in building the right foundation for a long lasting and successful business. Name is so powerful that it can antagonize the success of a business or product. Some business only started doing well when the name was changed. Those businesses could have done well at the beginning, if the right name has been given to it. If you need to change your business name, organization name, personal name go ahead now.

Your name is your brand, your name is your selling point, your name is the jackpot. Always go for the right name.

4. RIGHT STRUCTURE

The right structure is the foundation for a good business. The structure is the right pattern of positional and operational setting of the organization. Putting the right structure in place put the business on the right track of success. A good structure saves a business from been ruptured, and a good structure is the way to a good system. Without a good structure a good system will not delivered to its full capacity. The structure is the order of position and operation. It's also the hierarchy of position and function in the organization.

5. RIGHT SYSTEM

System is a pattern in which a thing is done. It is an organize scheme or method through which operation is run on a daily basis. You need a system on ground. System and structure work hand in hand to support the maximum delivery of the business. Good structure is the way to good system. A system is the pattern that has been designed and automated for the business to run on. The right system helps the business to run well on day to day activities without having to change the pattern of operation from time to time. A good system make you go to bed and watch the business repeat it day to day operation successfully.

6. RIGHT LEADERSHIP

It takes a leader to turn a great idea to a great business. The right leader knows what to do to get the best result possible. He sees the future no one sees, and move in confidence in the direction of where he is going. Just the way a good football team needs the right coach to guide it to win a trophy, a good business idea need the right leader to take it through. The right leadership is always discovered to be the forces behind the success of many great organizations. It takes a leader to see the end of the business from the beginning and to keep the faith of the staff and the business alive when the going gets tough. Get the right leader or be the right leader.

7. RIGHT FUND

Start your business with a clean fund. Don't start business with accursed money. Accursed money is stolen money. *Don't kill it before you start it.* Accursed money is a polluted offering that will eventually destroy the future of the business. It may succeed at the beginning, but the end will not go well. Don't just try it.

Up, sanctify the people, and say, sanctify yourselves against tomorrow: for thus saith the LORD God of Israel, [There is] an accursed thing in the midst of thee, O Israel: thou canst not stand before thine enemies, until ye take away the accursed thing from among you. Josh 7:13.

You just can't be praying to God when there is a problem with the fund that was invested to start the business. God will not be able to do anything about it than to reveal to you the source of the problem and the correction you need to make.

The imminent truth is that when you do business with a stolen fund for example; expect people to steal your products or goods. Accursed money will make whatever is done of it to become accursed. Don't use accursed money to start your business, it will ruin the business. Any money illegally gotten is accursed.

8. RIGHT TEAM/STAFF

The wrong people in the right business will crash it, the right people in the right business will move it forward. Some businesses that are meant to be thriving has nosedived because of the passionless and wrong people involved in it. If you have a good business idea with everything needed take your time to build your team. A good team is the driving force behind the progress of every organization. So, get a consultation before you get the people that will be involved in day to day running of the business.

What has light got to do with darkness? Wrong people are like darkness to the business. Don't follow your instinct alone, get advice and make research about everyone you add as part of the vision. If you employ a vision killer, they will end up killing the vision and walking away.

9. RIGHT KNOWLEDGE

Every business has it peculiar strategy and pattern. And so you need to go for the right information and knowledge that is necessary to turn the business around. If you have not been trained, get the training necessary for the delivery of the business. Get resources, mentorship and learn the trade.

Knowledge is one of the key to profit, growth and continuity of the business. Any business you have not acquired at least 80 percent knowledge necessary to execute it well, it is better you don't start it. Ignorance destroys, knowledge builds.

Through wisdom is an house builded; and by understanding it is established: And by knowledge shall the chambers be filled with all precious and pleasant riches. Prov. 24:3-4

Don't start the business on the platform of low skill and knowledge, or else it may not grow as fast as expected. Get adequate knowledge for adequate result. Adequate knowledge will empower you to take the business to the next level.

However, every business owners needs continuous acquisition of skills and knowledge to keep it growing. Right knowledge, with right application, with the prayer of faith will take the business to it desired haven. Success comes in business when relevant measures have been taken.

10. RIGHT BUSINESS PLAN

Make a good plan before venturing into any business. Plan every aspect of the business e.g from packaging to branding, to marketing, to customer service operation, record keeping, employing staff etc. Take time to seat down and draw a plan, design a structure, set a goal, write out your vision, mission, a business core values.

Plan for the business success on paper to get a clear picture of what you are venturing into.

Planning means taking the right step in ensuring the success of something through designing the path and pattern it will follow to succeed.

Planning is the step by step guide to the actualization of dream. The steps the idea will follow to be realized. It helps you to know who and what to carry along in the realization of a vision. How you want to start and where you want to start, with how much you need to start. Planning entails writing down the starting point, the middle and the end. Planning will help you to see your business through.

11. RIGHT BUSINESS LOCATION

Business location is also important for the success of the business. The geographic location is the soil that will facilitate the speed of growth and expansion of the business. Just the way every plant seed cannot be planted anywhere. There is a right soil for every seed to survive. The terrain mango seed will survive, that is not the terrain apple seed will not survive. Every business cannot thrive in every geographic location.

Some business dies within a year or two of starting it because it was wrongly located. Your business cannot be located just anywhere. The kind of business you want to go into determines the kind of location you must situate the business. You can't set up a school in an industrial location. Find out about the location before you settle down there. Ask questions about your location and also pray for a clear leading, like how secure the place is, and the beauty of the location for your business. Pray about the location. *He said, In all thy ways acknowledge him, and he shall direct thy paths. Prov. 3:6.* God is willing to direct your path in everything you inquire of him.

Man was created to live on the earth, while fish lives in the water. If man tries to change the order of location, he may not survive for long.

Location determines allocation. The right business location will connect you to the right people needed to make the business achieve it vision and mission, and the right market to sell the idea.

12. RIGHT KINGDOM INVESTMENT

Every business is a soul entity. You must understand this well and key into it. Every organization must have a pulse for kingdom investment; the first kingdom investment of every business is tithe. It is commanded for business to experience an open heaven.

Bring ye all the tithes into the storehouse, that there may be meat in mine house, and prove me now herewith, saith the LORD of hosts, if I will not open you the windows of heaven, and pour you out a blessing, that [there shall] not [be room] enough [to receive it]. And I will rebuke the devourer for your sakes, and he shall not destroy the fruits of your ground; neither shall your vine cast her fruit before the time in the field, saith the LORD of hosts. And all nations shall call you blessed: for ye shall be a delightsome land, saith the LORD of hosts. Malachi 3:10-12

This is the sustenance of any business established in righteousness. It is commanded with conditions of blessings, security and global acceptance for the business and organizational benefits. God commanded tithe, and he will watch over his word to perform it in your business.

The second area of investment is investing in a noble course in the house of God. Haggai 1: 3-8. Support in building the house of the Lord, God is pleased with this noble act. They are spiritual investment that commands God's blessings upon a business. The business cannot remain at the same level, if they do this faithfully.

Thirdly, investing in community development project, will give the business ground and good record in it environment.

13. KICKSTARTING AT YOUR SIZE

Do not despise the days of little beginning...your beginning may be small, but your end will be great.

Every giant was born a baby. Every elephant was born as a calf, but in the process of time, as they are been fed and nurtured, they grew bigger and bigger, till they formed into a giant size. Every business carries the seed of greatness. But a seed will first be sown and die and break-forth from the ground and begin to grow and bear fruit. That is how it is in business. There is nothing wrong in starting small. Every great thing starts small. So, take it one step at a time. Don't go and borrow huge money to start a business you are just venturing into, unless you have consulted with professionals and expert who are ready to help you to achieve your dream.

Every business grows over time. Any area you are facing challenges in business, seat down and do reviews, evaluate, ask question, pray and find out what could have caused the challenge you are experiencing now and make the proper correction.

Don't be discouraged you are starting small, start with what you have and plan and manage it well, with the help and leading of God, there will be breakthrough. God will bring you enlargement from one level to the other. So, don't stop what you have started, pause, pray, make new plans and forge ahead.

Any size you have the capacity to start and manage well is your small beginning.

14. RIGHT PRAYER FOR BUSINESS SUCCESS

He will: Grant thee according to thine own heart, and fulfil all thy counsel. We will rejoice in thy salvation, and in the name of our God **we will set up [our] banners:** *the LORD fulfil all thy petitions. Psalm 20:4,5.*

God has a reason why He said; open your mouth wide and I will fill it. When God created the heavens and the earth, the earth was void, nothing was in it. The first thing God called forth is light. The earth was covered with darkness, if it has remained in darkness; nothing would be in existence till now. Darkness kills, steals and destroy good things. So God evacuated darkness that men may be in existence.

God does not stop at creating men; He called the things needed for fruitfulness of the earth. As he calls them, he sees them and they were good. The word of God, filled up the earth. Likewise, God is waiting for the word of your mouth to fill your business with blessings.

A person will be satisfied with good from the fruit of his words, and the work of his hands will be rendered to him. Prov. 12:14

28

From the fruit of a person's mouth his stomach is satisfied, with the product of his lips is he satisfied. Death and life are in the power of the tongue, and those who love its use will eat its fruit. Prov. 18:20-21.

Your words are the fruit and dews that will rest upon your business and give it life. A dead business has no hope until it is resurrected through prayers.

15. RIGHT TIMING

And of the children of Issachar, [which were men] that had understanding of the times, to know what Israel ought to do; the heads of them [were] two hundred; and all their brethren [were] at their commandment.1Chr 12:32.

There is time to bring out every purpose. Time affect the existence of everything either positively or negatively. When events happen at the right time, it get people's support, but at the wrong time it get sympathy. Everything has it best time to manifest. The right time brings the best result. Time is life, a business born at the right time will experience acceptance. Try to take your time to launch out at the right time.

Other Things To Note
1. Pay your staff promptly.
2. Avoid shortcuts.
3. Avoid bribery and corrupt practices.
4. Keep your hands and business clean.
5. Separate from wrong association.
6. Deliver quality services and products.
7. Get your target market right.
8. Create a unique selling structure.

CHAPTER 2

NINETEEN REASONS FOR BUSINESS FAILURE

Many businesses close down day by day, week by week, month by month. Business failure is like when the break of a car fails, the car will head for a crash. Most times when car break fail, there is no remedy than for the car to crash and possible the driver is the first victim of casualty.

1. **Lack of vision:**

   Where [there is] no vision, the people perish: but he that keepeth the law, happy [is] he. Prov. 29:18

   Vision means to see, to create a glorious picture for your future. Vision inspires passion and drive to succeed. Vision gives you the courage to go on. And where there is no vision, the will be division. Vision is the picture of the future of that business. It is the destination. If you don't know your destination, you don't have a future.

2. **Lack of experience:**

   Many business fails, because the business man lack the key experience and basic knowledge to grow the business. Knowledge is a force of progress. Without knowledge and experience, the vision will end a disaster. You can't venture into what you don't have adequate knowledge to do. Experience they say is the best teacher.

3. **Lack of sufficient capital:**

   Some business needs lot of running cost to be able to make enough profit and pay their workforce. If such business lacks sufficient funds, the business will not have the power to carry on. And most staffs will be cut off. When the flow of fund has ceased, the business will shut down.

4. **Lack of financial management skill:**

   It is easier to spend money than to make it. You must learn how to manage the money when it comes in, so that it will not be underutilize or used for the wrong purpose.

   Good financial management skills entails you understand the business cash flow pattern, you know when to spend and when to earn. You understand the economic terrain of your business environment, and you have a good book keeping record.

5. **Lack of commitment:**

   Every business needs committed folks, someone with a driving force to drive the business through good times and bad times. Many business owners are not sold out to the business they said they believed in.

6. **Lack of helpers:**

   Helpers in business are those who are skilled and willing to help the business to achieve his goals and objective. Every business needs helpers. Helpers are eager and zealous people with total determination to take the business from the ground level to the top. Helpers go extra-mile for the business to succeed. Helpers will put in what it takes, there time, resources, talent and all the can do in their power to make sure the business becomes great. Helpers can be an employee, a client or even a stranger with the interest of the business at heart. If helpers are lacking, some business will suffer set back.

7. **Lack of purpose:**
   What is the purpose why the business was established? There is a purpose for establishing any venture. Purpose is the reason for a thing. What does it stand to benefit humanity? The purpose must be clear and always set in the picture of the mission of the business.

8. **Wrong location:**
   Wrong location is like a bad luck. A business situated in a wrong business location will not grow the way it is meant to grow. Right location is needed to boost the sales and success of a business. The nature of your business will determine the location you sort for the business.

   Wrong location is like planting a seed on the rock, it will not survive on the hard stone and the heat of the sun will dry up the seed.

9. **Extravagant lifestyle:**
   Spending the business money without considering the future of the business will cause failure. No matter the profit the business is making, it is not appropriate to be frugal in spending. If you use the business fund to fulfill

your frugal lifestyle and satisfy all your worldly pleasure, soon the business will close down. Spend wisely and consider the future of the business.

10. Embezzlement and stealing:

Embezzlement and stealing will kill the business fast. Embezzlement is the ruin of any business. It is a situation where some key folks of the organization are stealing money behind the scene. A business that is destined to be great will die if it is surrounded by thieves and robbers.

Often times, embezzlement and stealing is not just by one person, but by few parasite among the staff, who has seen this as a way of making it fast and eventually sending the business into a bankruptcy.

11. Following Band wagon effect:

Don't do business because it is the reigning trend. A bandwagon effect is when a business is the talk of the town and everyone is going into it because of the fast profit or the much interest the business is spinning in, most times people who rushed into the business will end up crashing in the business.

12. Wrong business advice:

It is not everybody that is qualified to be your business adviser. Wrong adviser will give an advice that will end the business in loss. Wrong business investment and wrong business decision equals to business failure. A good business adviser is the lifeline of a business.

[Every] purpose is established by counsel: and with good advice make

war. Prov 20:18.

You must consider the person that you are taking your advice from. It must be an experience person and a person who has your interest at heart.

13. Getting chicken to do eagles job:

Eagles and chicken are birds with different strength, characters and makeup. What eagles can do, chicken does not have the ability for it. Eagles don't eat what chickens eat, eagles don't think the way chicken think, eagles soars in the air while chicken walk on the ground. Eagles are birds with great vision and insights while chicken are visionless birds.

Many documentaries has been done on eagles because of its unique abilities, skills and valor. Only few documentaries are done on chicken. People will prefer documentary on eagles to chicken.

Getting chicken to do eagles job simply means getting a less qualified person to do a professional work. It will kill the business. In business, let the eagles do eagles job, while the chicken focus on their jobs, it makes everything go smoothly.

14. Overstaffing and understaffing:

Knowing the number of people to employ per time is important, and knowing how to shed staff or to add more hands is important. Overstaffing will make the company to be spending more than necessary on the employees. When there are too many staff, there will be too many wages being paid monthly from the profit of the company and that can affect the fund and finance of the company.

Understaffing is getting few people to do so many people's work. A situation when two people are doing the work of ten people will slow production, will drag down supply and the company will be unable to meet demands.

15. Violating business principles

If one of the principles of the business is to hire strictly qualified staff and out of compromise, the human resource unit hired someone not qualified for the job in the bid to cut cost, it can affect the quality of delivery.

Comprising company standard of operation and delivery can cause a rupture in the foundation of success that has been laid.

Then if the company has a policy of closing doors to creditors, and they eventually open doors to strategy that encourage buy now pay later without an effective strategy to get the money of the goods and services back, it will affect the business negative.

16. Lack of structure:

A business without a structure will soon rupture. Structure helps business to manage it growth and progress without collapsing the system. It is the structure that holds the system together.

17. Lawsuits and court cases:

Business soon close down when it's going out of one case and entering another, if eventually the company lose a major case that may be the downfall of that business.

There was a big organization that used to generates millions of naira daily, but due to loss of court case to one of their clients they were asked to close down. And the business was closed down without consideration by the state government.

18. Lack of innovation

New trend will affect a company that lacks innovation to meet up with the latest trend. A company that maintains her outdated style of delivery and product packaging will soon lost her customers to company that has come out with an innovation that will capture the market.

Innovation must be embraced, must be timely, must be up to date, must be in line with the trend, for total acceptability. Timely innovation brings motivation among the staff and promotion for the business.

19. Lack of Motivation:

You need to remain motivated to remain relevant in hard times. Motivation is the fuel that keeps the engine running. Motivation is the power to keep going when things are getting out of hands. Motivation is a driving force. When motivation dies everything dies.

CHAPTER 3

STAGES OF BUSINESS

He hath made every [thing] beautiful in his time: also he hath set the world in their heart… Eccl 3:11a

Every business has stages of development just like fetus in the womb. Stages of business development must not be overlooked, because each stage has its own unique challenges and lessons. Every business stage creates a better platform for the business to thrive. And each stage contribute to the solid standing of the business among it pears. Understand that every business undergo this stage at different time frame and duration. Business varies from people to people, from vision to vision, from products to product. So every business has its own stage of maturity into a global success. However each of these stages is required to plan, plant, plow and proceed the growth of the business till it becomes a generational phenomenon.

These Are The Stages Business Undergo

It is important you know the stage your business is per time, and the time frame it is meant to be there before it moves to the next phase. And ensure you don't over stay in a particular business phase, except there is a tangible reason that keeps the business down. However, every business must pass these stages to solidify and grow into that business of your dream.

As a leader, with good strategic plans on paper, you should know the stage the business is per time.

Conception

The first stage is when the business idea is conceived. It is a stage of discovery of a new idea. You developed the desire to give birth to an idea that will bless humanity and be a channel of financial stream to you and people.

At stage of conception, you settle down on the choice of doing one business anyway. Every stage requires praying through and asking the right question.

Incubation

Incubation stage is the stage of preparation, acquisition, researching, doing findings and learning about the business, and how to go about it. The idea is processed, evaluated, scrutinized and weighed. You don't enter a business you know nothing or less about just because you have gotten an idea, or you see people doing it. You must have at least eighty percent knowledge on what you want to do. This stage helps you to know the dos and don'ts of the business. What it takes to start, to survive and to make it. It is a stage you learn the how, what, when, where and who are needed.

Planning

This is the stage you draw a business plan. The business comes to the paper. You give the business an identity to have a pathway.

You plan for the location, number of people needed to carry the vision, write the vision, write the business plan, all the equipments, tools and facilities needed, and cost of all the things needed. How to source for fund, and then break it down to the fund you visibly have access to.

Delivery Stage
The business comes into existence at this stage. This is the time the business is given birth to and the eyes of all see the new baby. Every business running today has gone through all this stages. This is the point the dream becomes a reality to tend. This is also the nursing stage, you nurture the business till it moves to the next stage where it begins to crawl.

Crawling Stage
It is the stage of awareness. People getting to know the business exists. The company is doing everything to get people to know what they offer and what they stand for. This is a stage of gradual progress.

Walking Stage
The business is gaining some measure of recognition at this stage, the product and service are been tested, and customers are not gradually recognizing it, appreciating it and recommending it. This is what moves it to the next stage.

Running Stage
The business is doing well at this stage. Many businesses take longer to get to the stage where the business makes enough sales on a daily basis to meet up the daily expenses of the company. What brings business to this stage is determination

and passion, because most businesses fail before getting here. If the company maintaining the key that is turning customer in and determination, the business will be booming and that will launch it to the stage I call the flying stage.

Flying Stage:
The business has gained ground at this stage. It has already being accepted, recognized and has a voice of its own. It has become a brand product in the market. This is the stage the business fully picks up as you desire, and begins to flourish even beyond your expectation.

Soaring Stage:
This is a stage of stability. The system and structure has been fully established and it is working well. Sales at this stage are like a flowing river. Customers can't wait to get the purchase done. This is the stage where all things are working in the favor of the business and it is already stabilize. This is the stage the business grows and expands in leaps and bound. The progress you are making becomes progressive on a daily basis. The economic atmosphere and the market and sales all favor the business.

STATES OF BUSINESS

This business situation will help you to drive your business out of the situation you don't want to the level you want.

Flourishing business
This is a business with an autopilot structure; whoever comes on board just fit in to continue the process of success established in the business, rather the business makes you

successful. The business is stable and doing well on its own. It is a business of the people that enjoys the flow of grace supernaturally.

Successful business
It is a business that good plan and system is helping to prosper. If the right person at the center is out, the business may begin to come down until there is a quick adjustment.

Rising and falling business
It will do well today and it will come down tomorrow, with or without a particular reason. Some of these businesses are seasonal. In their season they do well, off their season they do worse. And some businesses are not affected seasons, but other economic factors.

Business in this category will be experiencing on and off until something is done to cushion the problem. It will just require the right and skill person to take over and in no time it will come back.

Dead business
It is a business that is spiritually dead, though physically it is existing and there is no more patronage. It is obvious that the glory has departed. Nothing meaningful is happening in the business, it is the shadow of itself. Business in this category needs the touch of God to revive it. Don't give up on business at this states, get all the expertise necessary to revive it. Give it whatever it will take to bring back the glory and it will be worth it at the end.

Dark business

This is an illegal business. Whether it is doing well or doing badly. The foundation is not right, the people doing it are not right. It is just a dark business all the way.

Illegal business is dubious and has great consequences at the end.

CHAPTER 4

DON'T GIVE UP ON THAT BUSINESS YET

If you faint in the day of trouble, your strength is small! Prov 24:10

There is hope for that business again. Giving up is not the solution. Don't think you are not competent to revive that business. All your effort may not have yielded any meaningful outcome, but here is the solution now, *prayer.*

For there is hope of a tree, if it be cut down, that it will sprout again, and that the tender branch thereof will not cease. Though the root thereof wax old in the earth, and the stock thereof die in the ground; [Yet] through the scent of water it will bud, and bring forth boughs like a plant. Job 14:7-9.

Be rest assured that there is hope, the business will bounce back. If the business has failed, it can still succeed. Failure is not a full stop, it is a coma, learn what you don't know and try again. Don't give up, start all over. You are born for success, you are not a failure. You will surely succeed if you take the challenge to God through prayer and take time to review necessary causes of the failure. You are responsible to restore the glory of the business.

Whatsoever thy hand findeth to do, do [it] with thy might; for [there is] no work, nor device, nor knowledge, nor wisdom, in the grave, whither thou goest. Eccl 9:10

Whatever your hands find to do, do it with all your might; put in all it takes to keep it alive. Many people's destiny depend on the success of your business, without that business they will go through moment of hardship in life, but it is through that business some will earn wages, some will find succor, some will be a channel of distribution of the goods and passage of the service. Business is life; it gives hope to many people and takes care of many families and sustains the economy of a nation. Persevere to see it survive.

What you have in your hand is a seed, don't let it die, it is an opportunity don't let it slip away. Even if you will start another one, you can give that one in your hand at the moment life. Every seed needs time to be nurtured, to be pruned so that it can survive. In every seed lies millions of fruits, in every business lies million of opportunity.

What to do?

1. **Pray revelational prayers:**
    Call unto me, and I will answer thee, and shew thee great and mighty things, which thou knowest not. Jer. 33:3

    God will show you the problem and also the solution to the challenges you are facing in that business. All he requires from you is a time with him on that business. God intervene in the affair of his people through prayer of faith. Prayer is simply calling the attention of God to what you are doing. God is the only wise God, he stores up knowledge, and nothing is too hard for him to do.

When you engage him, he intervenes with his power and wisdom.

2. Be sensitive to what God will lead you to do:

His mother saith unto the servants, Whatsoever he saith unto you, do . John 2:5

God is a solution provider and an instructor. When you have prayed to God expect his instruction or direction through many of his medium of communication, dream, vision, speaking through the Holy Spirit, read more in the prayer section below. Whatever he reveals or tells you to do, do it without analyzing it that is the key to success.

3. Learn more about the business:

Study to shew thyself approved unto God, a workman that needeth not to be ashamed, rightly dividing the word of truth. 2Tim 2:15

The more you know about the business, the better you become in managing the business. Sometimes people experience failure because they have less than five percent knowledge of the business, though they have the zeal and resources, but no knowledge, without knowledge, resources will come to waste, and passion will turn to frustration. Go and learn more professional way of going about the business, acquire more skill, read more books, get video tutorial on how the business is done. You will learn loads of new thing that will help you to stand on your feet and keep the business going.

4. **Get a mentor in the area of the business:**
    Where no counsel [is], the people fall: but in the multitude of counsellors [there is] safety. Prov 11:14

    Get mentorship from those who are doing the same business and have made an headway. Transfer of knowledge is transfer of blessing. If they pass on their knowledge to you, they have given you a new dimension of power to carry on and succeed in that business.

5. **Review your system**
    Check out the system to see where there is a fracture in the system and fix it right away.

CHAPTER 5

THE FORCE OF CONFESSION

For by thy words thou shalt be justified, and by thy words thou shalt be condemned. Matt 12:37

Confession is to a business what sun is to a plant. Confession is a life giving declaration over a business. A business will survive as long as it is watered with the word of life. What you say is what you see. It is important you say what you want to see. It is calling those things that were not as if they were. There is power in the word of your mouth. Your declaration is your expectation; God honors the true word of your heart to back it up with manifestation.

Confession has the power to bring to pass every word of declaration according to the genuine desires of your heart. Confession is the innate ability God created with us along himself.

A man's belly shall be satisfied with the fruit of his mouth; [and] with the increase of his lips shall he be filled. Death and life [are] in the power of the tongue: and they that love it shall eat the fruit thereof. Prov. 18:20-21.

Don't kill your business with your mouth. Don't release words of death into that business, rather release word of life into it. You shall have what you say.

You are a spiritual entity; God has made you so, so that you can have in-depth understanding of life and things. God himself want you to confess what you desire to see over your life and business in faith.

Say ye to the righteous, that [it shall be] well [with him]: for they shall eat the fruit of their doings. Isa 3:10

Some blessings and expectation will not come to pass until it is constantly confessed and enforced. And it is the duty of every individual to engage the power of life and death in their tongue, to uproot what they don't want to see and to enforce what they expect to see on a daily basis.

STRENGTH OF CONFESSION:

1. **The Word Of God:**
    Where the word of the king is there is power. Eccl. 8:4. The strength of your confession lies in the power of God's word. God is the king of kings; however where the word of the king of king is there will be power and change. Let your confession agree with the word of God, and proceed from the word of God. The word of God is living water. Your business is a seed. The more of the word you water on your business, the more fruitful the business becomes. The word is life, the release of the word on the business, brings life into the business. Where God has released life, death cannot encroach.

2. The Spirit Of God:

And the earth was without form, and void; and darkness [was] upon the face of the deep. And the Spirit of God moved upon the face of the waters. And God said, Let there be light: and there was light. Gen. 1:2-3

The Spirit of the Lord is the performer. Whatever you say, needs certain force to get it done, and that is the Spirit of the Lord. When God spoke it takes his Spirit to make his word come to pass, the same Spirit is available for every believer. If you must say it and see it, you must be filled with the Spirit of the Lord.

3. Personal motivation:

Motivation is a powerful drive. If you are not motivated, you will be dehydrated. Motivation is a force that revives strength and courage in you. You need to stay motivated to keep believing in yourself. When motivation dies, courage will die, hope will dwindle, set back will set in. you must make sure your motivation tank is filled with the hope of the promises of God's word.

How to be filled with the Spirit of the Lord

a. Be Saved: John 1:12

The mystery of salvation is that it comes through confession, Rom. 10:9-10, after believing that Jesus died for you and he has been made your Lord and Savior. Salvation bridges the gap between man and God.

49

b. Ask for baptism of the Spirit: Luke 11:13

For every one that asketh receiveth; and he that seeketh findeth; and to him that knocketh it shall be opened. If a son shall ask bread of any of you that is a father, will he give him a stone? or if [he ask] a fish, will he for a fish give him a serpent? Or if he shall ask an egg, will he offer him a scorpion? If ye then, being evil, know how to give good gifts unto your children: how much more shall [your] heavenly Father give the Holy Spirit to them that ask him? Luke 11:10-13

God has assured to give anyone that asked from a genuine heart. So go into three days fasting and ask God for it, and God will fulfill his word by feeling you with Holy Spirit.

4. Your faith:

That your faith should not stand in the wisdom of men, but in the power of God. 1Cor 2:5

Faith is a spiritual converter that converts spiritual substance into physical substance. The power of faith released into a situation turns things around for good. God works through faith, faith is evidence of your expectation and your confidence in the ability of God that he is able to do whatever is said. Faith is the boldness in the possibility of God's ability to bring expectation and declaration to pass.

CHAPTER 6

PRINCIPLE OF BUSINESS EXPLOSION

When the right product, meet the right people, through the right channel, at the right time, with your faith steady, then explosion begins.

The dream of every business is not only to get their product and services seen, but to take over the market. A product and service becomes a household name when explosion takes place. Explosion makes enlargement possible. It makes expansion easy and makes way for more profit, and resources to help the business grow as dreamt.

Business explosion is when your business experience sudden breakthrough in the market place whereby the attention of everyone is suddenly turned to your product and service for patronage and people are spreading the goodnews about the beauty of the products and services. Business explosion is not by chance, it is by rightly and timely action. God wants every business to breakthrough. God owns what you have. You own what God has. All that is God are yours. When your business is connected to the threshold of God, it will enjoy the flow of favor, favor brings acceptance by everyone. God wants every of your genuine business endeavor to be successful. When your business experience breakthrough it will open other doors relevant for your enlargement. It is the business explosion that makes you a blessing.

1. **RIGHT/ PRODUCT AND SERVICE**

    Don't compromise the standard and quality of the product you offer. People need quality goods and services. People want to be part of the product testimony, you have to understand that. So you make them belong by the quality and standard of the product you offer.

2. **CREATIVE AND ACTIVE AWARENESS**

    Create awareness as much as possible and through any means available. People get to know what you sell, before they can buy into what you sell. Awareness means showcasing the product to the public and makes known to the people the benefit of the product. You must expose and explain it.

    They want to see it and they want to know what it does, how it can benefit and profit them. If they see it and don't know it benefit, that is half awareness. Let people be able to tell others what the product will do for them. Advertise, market, talk about it, everywhere, every time. It goes a long way. Do it every day, every night and at every opportunity you find.

3. **GOOD BRANDING**

    Your brand will speak so much of your product. Brand is the life of the product. As you know, it involves product name, product quality, product durability, product integrity, and product eternal comfort to the people.
    Brand it right. It gives the product volume, depth, and take it to places where the company may not reach at a time.

4. BENEFIT OF DOUBT

Give them the value for money. Give them assurance that they will enjoy the product and the warranty on the product. People feel secure when they have warranty on goods purchased.

5. EXERCISE TOTAL FAITH

Faith does not exercise limitation. Faith is exercising boldness and confidence in what God can do in that business. Faith delivers by power. Faith here means to exercise the deposit of the power of God that makes things work in you. Power controls the force of nature, to give way to the force of light. And faith is the force of light.

Walk in faith, not in fear or doubt. Faith don't see obstacles, it sees possibilities. Put on your faith jacket in the name of Jesus. The host of heaven is waiting to back you up, as soon as you begin to exercise your faith. Faith will bring you out of your shell. Break the shell completely and come out totally.

6. EXPAND YOUR TENTACLES

Give out franchise; create a free or paid training platform for your product and service to spread out. Recruit agents to spread the good news of your product and services.

7. TITHING FOR THE BUSINESS:

Bring ye all the tithes into the storehouse, that there may be meat in mine house, and prove me now herewith, saith the LORD of hosts, if I will not open you the windows of heaven, and pour you out a blessing, that [there shall] not [be room] enough [to receive it]. And I will rebuke the devourer for your sakes, and he shall not destroy the fruits of your ground; neither shall your vine cast her fruit before the time in the field, saith the LORD of hosts. And all nations shall call you blessed: for ye shall be a delightsome land, saith the LORD of hosts. Mal. 3:10-12

Tithe is commanded by God. Your tithe is the ten percent of your business profit. What you make as gain, put it all together, and remove the ten percent as God's own. Take it to a church of God and give it to God. It is a divine instruction backed with blessing.

8. PRAY FOR EXPLOSION:

Every action you take works together to deliver your expectation. Prayer is an avenue to reach for spiritual impartation of God's anointing of explosion over the business. Expect explosion and pray for explosion. Prayer is an evidence of your expectation for what you are asking for. God however, grants men's expectation without fail.

There is different between confession and prayer. When you confess you are making a declaration but when pray you a making a request. Both of them are powerful, but prayer do much more than request, prayer open closed doors, it removes barriers and obstacles, it destroy the works of darkness and brings freedom.

CHAPTER 7

WHY THE BUSINESS NEEDS PRAYER

Everything needs certain spiritual input and sacrifice to keep thriving, which one of it is prayer. Prayer is a spiritual exercise that you don't require any one to do for you, you can undertake a prayer task on your own. Every venture, organization, business or ministry, thrives on supernatural backing. The most guaranteed backing is the backing of God. Whatever God is behind, cannot collapse.

The LORD thy God in the midst of thee [is] mighty; he will save, he will rejoice over thee with joy; he will rest in his love, he will joy over thee with singing. Zeph 3:17

It is a mark of submission to God to take over as the higher authority, who can help you to achieve any level of your dream in that business. The ability of God is infinite, he prepare rains for the earth, the same way he will prepare customers for the business, he makes grass to grow on the mountain. That is seemingly unimaginable. Mountain is like a solid stone, that is not where grass are meant to grow, but by his unique power, it makes it possible for grass to grow on the mountain to give food to his creatures. So he will make the business to grow in the midst of harsh economic condition breaking any barrier for the business to succeed.

However, God will do that to those who have come to trust on him, and believe in his ability only. If the living God is your father, I think He deserves to be given this honor in your business.

Why The Business Needs Prayer

1. **The business is an entity: Isaiah 27:2-3**
   In that day sing ye unto her, A vineyard of red wine. I the LORD do keep it; I will water it every moment: lest [any] hurt it, I will keep it night and day. Isa 27:2-3

   The business is like an entity. Every business is like a plant that has to be watered, fertilized, nurtured, and taken care. The way weeding is needed in the farm around certain plant so that the weed will not stagnate the growth, prayer is needed around your business so that the enemy will not shock the business and all your investment in it will yield profit and not loses.

2. **It needs divine backup: Exod. 33:14**
   And he said, My presence shall go [with thee], and I will give thee rest. Exod 33:14

   Every business needs divine backup. Divine backup will guarantee divine favor and divine connection. When God is in the business, the business will flourish. The presence of God is needed in the business to experience rest in the business.

3. **It is located in an environment: Zech. 1: 18-21.**

   Every business is located in certain geographical location, while every area has it spiritual do's and don'ts. There are territorial powers and spirit, there are altars, there are spiritual gates of darkness that has to be lifted if need be for you to gain dominion over the location and do well.

4. **It needs financial provision: Phil. 4:19.**

   But my God shall supply all your need according to his riches in glory by Christ Jesus. Phil 4:19

   Many businesses need financial provision. Financial provision is also the same as divine provision. Many company run on loan of some sort, but if you invite God through fervent prayer, He will send help to the business in a medium you don't expect. God don't operate with men's wisdom, His wisdom is higher than that of men and this is enough to solve the problem of men.

5. **There are forces who don't want the business to succeed:**

   For we wrestle not against flesh and blood, but against principalities, against powers, against the rulers of the darkness of this world, against spiritual wickedness in high [places]. Eph 6:12

   The business environment today is physically and spiritually tense. It take the strong to take charge of the environment. We are in the days men consult different source to keep their business on top. Those are forces you don't know. If you are going to succeed in the business environment today, you must understand that there are forces you may need to contend with at one point or the other, and prepare your weapons of warfare ahead. There are many forces who don't want that business to succeed beyond the level it is now. You need to silence them with the authority in Jesus name Phil. 2:9-11, and the force of prayer.

6. **To take charge of your spiritual and physical business environment: Luke 10:19**
Jesus has given you the mandate to occupy till he comes. You can take charge without power. He said, I give unto you power to tread on serpent, scorpion and all the powers of the enemy. Prayer is the activation key of power.

7. **To control the direction of the business sales:**
You can use the force of prayer to direct the sail of the business.

Sources people depend on for success

1. **God:**
Very few people depend on God. Whoever depends on God must show to God that he does depend on him. God will definitely work with those who depend on him for the business to succeed.

2. **Satanic backup:**

58

There are people who go into occultism, worship one idol or the other just to have success. They make sacrifice in secret places on altars just to get satanic backup.

3. **Brain work:**

    Some people believe in their capacity and brain work. They believe strategies, goal setting and planning is what makes a business succeed. Actually all this contribute to business success, none of this can be ruled out, but the business power today know that as much as all these things are important, their also spiritual back up to aid in the marketability and breakthrough of their products and services.

4. **Some people:**

    Those who depend on people believes that it is the people you know that matters, believing that when you know people in good position, you can find help with them and arise. Some sect also believes in getting good resource and skill people to run the business. They can change as many managers, directors etc as possible just to get the right person to get the business up. People can fail, people can die, people cannot do beyond their limit. Only God can make every dream come through in a way you least expect.

STAGE TWO
PRAYER FOR NEW BUSINESS ESTABLISHMENT

In the name of the Lord we will **set up our banners**...*Psalm 20:5b*

CHAPTER 8

HOW TO BEGIN

Everything has a right process, when you follow the due process, you will get the due result in no time. I need to walk you through this prayer process so that your heavens can be open and God can hear you.

Now we know that God heareth not sinners: but if any man be a worshipper of God, and doeth his will, him he heareth. John 9:31

When God hears you, it is an assurance that what you have asked has been settled. You are praying to God because it is God that answers prayer, and he delights in hearing your prayers.

The sacrifice of the wicked [is] an abomination to the LORD: but the prayer of the upright [is] his delight. Prov. 15:8.

How beautiful is the prayer of the son to the father, He will gladly receive it and proof that he is God. Prayer however turns things around. Every great venture start with prayer, anything that start on the pattern of God's will and prayer can hardly go wrong, as long as God is involved.

The process:
1. **Give your life to Jesus:**

Salvation is the foundation for intervention. Anyone that receives Jesus receives God. God takes delights in sons, not in strangers. If you are not in Christ you are a stranger to the covenant of promise. Salvation makes you a partaker of the promise.

Salvation comes by confessing Jesus Christ as your Lord and savior and forsaking your sinful life, and living based on the standard of God's word. Rom. 10:9-10, John 14:15.

2. **Begin to serve God:**
   You need to serve God to be known of God, you serve God through fellowship with the brethren. Join the company believer that gathers to God in truth and spirit, using the bible as a standard for their spiritual measure. Ps. 133:1-3

3. **Read the word daily: Joshua 1:8**
   This book of the law shall not depart out of thy mouth; but thou shalt meditate therein day and night, that thou mayest observe to do according to all that is written therein: for then thou shalt make thy way prosperous, and then thou shalt have good success. Josh 1:8

   The word of God is the source of divine wisdom for successful living, successful business, and successful relationship with man and God. However, it is not limited to that alone; it is the instrument of spiritual power for waging war against every opposition.

4. **Ask for the baptism of the Holy Spirit and Power.**

But ye shall receive power, after that the Holy Ghost is come upon you: Acts 1:8a

You need the Holy Spirit for instruction, direction, innovation, protection and divine business ideas. With the Holy Spirit comes power. Power makes your dominion to be real. No king reign without power.

5. **Engage Fasting: Matt. 17:21.**
    Fasting make you more spiritually potent. It makes your spiritual ability to manifest, and develop your spiritual stamina. With all this, you are ready to pray through.

6. **Discover the challenge you have in your business**
    The discovery of your challenge in business is the key to recovery. You can't recover from what you don't discover the source of it challenges. Discovery help you know what prayer and steps to take in order to get the right result.

    This discovery may be in the area of the business, or the area of your life. You may really be the challenge the business has. Your discovery will guide you to solution.

Prayer of salvation

Declare thus:

That if thou shalt confess with thy mouth the Lord Jesus, and shalt believe in thine heart that God hath raised him from the dead, thou shalt be saved. For with the heart man believeth unto righteousness; and with the mouth confession is made unto salvation. Rom 10:9.

Lord Jesus, look upon me and show me mercy, forgive all my sins and come into my life today. Save me, I accept you now as my personal Lord and Savior, ready to serve you to the end, release grace upon me in Jesus name.

Prayer of purging and sanctification

And he shall sit [as] a refiner and purifier of silver: and he shall purify the sons of Levi, and purge them as gold and silver, that they may offer unto the LORD an offering in righteousness. Mal 3:3.

1. Oh Lord, sanctify me with your blood in the name of Jesus.
2. Let your blood silence every voice that want to silence me in the name of Jesus.
3. Let your blood speak for me henceforth in the name of Jesus.
4. Oh Lord my father, purge me with your fire in the name of Jesus.
5. Every stranger in me, Holy Ghost fire purge them out in the name of Jesus.
6. Lay your hands on your hand and begin to say blood of Jesus sanctify my spirit soul and body. 7x.
7. Lay your hands on your hand and declare, Holy Ghost fire purge my spirit, soul and body. 7x.
8. Cleanse me completely from every pollution, defilement, covenants, curses in the name of Jesus.
9. Holy Ghost, perfect that which concerns me in Jesus name.

Prayer for Holy Ghost Baptism and Power

But ye shall receive power, after that the Holy Ghost is come upon you: and ye shall be witnesses unto me both in Jerusalem, and in all Judaea, and in Samaria, and unto the uttermost part of the earth. Acts 1:8.

Behold, I give unto you power to tread on serpents and scorpions, and over all the power of the enemy: and nothing shall by any means hurt you. Luke 10:19.

1. Father, I am ready to be filled with your Spirit, send your Spirit upon me to tabernacle in the name of Jesus.
2. Holy Spirit, I am available for you, I have clear the temple for you, come and fill my temple in the name of Jesus.
3. Heaven of Holy Ghost baptism open upon me in the name of Jesus.
4. Jesus Christ, fill me with the Holy Ghost and power in the name of Jesus.
5. Mantle of power fall upon me in the name of Jesus.

CHAPTER 9

PRAYER FOR BUSINESS SUCCESS

*Finally, brethren, pray for us, that the word of the Lord may have [free]
course, and be glorified, even as [it is] with you:
And that we may be delivered from unreasonable and wicked men: for all
[men] have not faith. 2Thess. 3:1-2*

Every success is spiritual in nature. God is the custodian of success, though he has embedded in men the ability to succeed if they obey and follow principles and precepts. However, prayer is the one of the major key of success. You cannot exempt spiritual input in your journey to succeed in your physical endeavour, your spiritual input is what pave way for the principles to find a ground to take root and bear fruit.

Principles without prayer input will lead to principal frustration. Nature is a force, business is an entity, to give room for this entity to thrive on the soil of nature; you need a force that will make the force of nature give way for the business to thrive.

Every right business deserves to do well. Prayer sustains. It is the right thing to start every venture with prayer and continue in prayer. In the present unfriendly economic situation in the world today, success is not easy to come by. Success however is a function of God's favor, not man's wishes, strategies or plans as such. No perfect plan can guarantee perfect success; it is only divine favor that can guarantee success beyond imagination. Men's strategy and planning fails when favor is missing. Where there is no favor, everything looks tough, but where there is favor, everything becomes easy. People troop to the corridor of favor, the way ants troop around honey. Divine favor is from God. When the favor of the Lord is upon a business all the way, it will enjoy success all the way. Little input will break forth into bigger testimony, while much input will break forth into much greater testimony.

Your business is a living entity that has an ear and as you declare the blessing upon it, it will rest on it forever. The water of the word must be sprinkled over the business, so that all hindrances, obstacles, limitation that can debar the success can be removed by the power of God.

Why You Need To Pray This Prayer
1. Prayer moves the hand of God to work on your behalf.
2. Prayer is a spiritual force that makes a way for business in tough times.
3. Prayer gives you dominion over your principal adversaries.
4. Prayer makes the business experience unstoppable progress.
5. Prayer facilitates success and testimonies.

Who Need This Prayer
1. If you always experience failure in what you do.
2. If you want to experience uncommon result in your business venture.
3. If you have invested much and seen little in return.

4. If you are having fear things may not turn out as planned.
5. If you have faith in the immeasurable ability of God.
6. If you are a true believer, who understand the power of prayer.

Scriptural declaration

Blessed [is] every one that feareth the LORD; that walketh in his ways. 2 For thou shalt eat the labour of thine hands: happy [shalt] thou [be], and [it shall be] well with thee. Psalm 128:1-2

But my horn shalt thou exalt like [the horn of] an unicorn: I shall be anointed with fresh oil. Ps 92:10

The righteous shall flourish like the palm tree: he shall grow like a cedar in Lebanon. Ps 92:12

Prayers

1. Mercy for business success, locate my business in Jesus name.
2. Anointing for business success, rest upon my business in Jesus name.
3. Any unnoticed event that may attack this business for failure, be aborted in Jesus name.
4. Every mistake that can happen to bring down my business, be revealed to me and aborted in Jesus Christ name.
5. The right ideas, that will enhance the success of this business per-time, be revealed to me in the name of Jesus.
6. The right people that will contribute to the success of this business, Holy Spirit bring them into this business in Jesus name.

7. Any wrong idea that will stampede and affect the growth and success of this business, I reject you, be exposed in the name of Jesus.

8. The power of God for success, rest upon (mention the name of the business) e.g Voice of Hope international, in Jesus name.

9. Every effect of wrong location over this business be nullified in Jesus name.

10. (Mention the name of the business) I open up your destiny for success, prosperity and breakthroughs in the name of Jesus.

11. (Mention the name of the business) if anyone calls you for evil, reject their voice in the name of Jesus.

12. (Mention the name of the business) you will not be manipulated in the name of Jesus.

13. (Mention the name of the business) you will get to your peak in the name of Jesus.

14. (Mention the name of the business) from this point on, I shake out from you every wrong people and things that is causing you setback, and I command by the power of the Holy Ghost, begin to attract right people and right things in the name of Jesus Christ.

15. (Mention the name of the business), I declare success over you in the name of Jesus.

CHAPTER 10

PRAYER FOR BUSINESS DEDICATION

And Solomon offered a sacrifice of peace offerings, which he offered unto the LORD, two and twenty thousand oxen, and an hundred and twenty thousand sheep. So the king and all the children of Israel dedicated the house of the LORD. 1Kgs 8:63

Dedication means to commit the business into God's hand. To acknowledge God in the establishment of the business, so that God can be the alpha and omega of the business. Anything dedicated to God has become sacred and untouchable to the devil and his agents.

Dedication also means to give honor to whom honor should be given. God deserves to be honored at the privilege of establishing an inspired business. God said, those who honor me I will honor. When you honor God through dedication of your new business, he receives the glory and sends you honor in return.

Every new thing therefore has to be dedicated to the Lord, so that he can be the head of such things. Whatever is not dedicated to God, may not enjoy the involvement of God. Dedication makes God readily part of the venture.

Reasons For Dedication

1. Start with God.
2. Sacred to God.
3. Blessing from God.
4. Backing from God.
5. Protection of God.

How To Dedicate

1. Invite a pastor or minister of God to the business office to pray there at the opening or after.
2. Get your workers or partners around for the prayer dedication.
3. Praise and worship God few minutes.
4. Exhortation for few minutes.
5. Praying and anointing the business location and facilities in the name of the Lord where the business will be officially dedicated to the Lord.

Note: You can also do the dedication yourself, if you have no clergy to do that for you, where you are.

Understand also that business can start small, in a house, shop, or any place that you find suitable. It is your business that adds value to the location, and then the location complements your business. You can also dedicate with just you, your wife and children and minister of God. Just let there be right witness.

Scripture to declare

Psalm 23, Psalm 24

Let the heaven of this business be open, let the Spirit of the living God overshadow this business, and let the glory of this business manifest. Let the light of this business begin to shine for everyone to see, let it become a delight to everyone that will see it, and experience lofty patronage in the name of Jesus. Let the glory of God rest upon the business, let the door ways of customers be opened now and let it bring everyone full satisfaction in the name of Jesus.

You (mention the business name) you are dedicated in the name of the Lord of host. In Jesus name you are established today by the power of the Holy-Ghost. Then you anoint your office and some of the facilities available for use.

Prayer of dedication
1. Thank you Jesus, for giving us this inspiration in the name of Jesus
2. Thank you Jesus, for making us give birth to this idea in Jesus name.
3. Thank you for this day in the name of Jesus.
4. Oh Lord, we have come to hand over this business to you, take it over in the name of Jesus.
5. The name of the Lord is a strong tower the righteous runs into it and is saved; I bring this business under the canopy of the name of the Lord.
6. Any problem that may arise against this business that will bring us losses, failure or bankruptcy, be exposed and terminated in Jesus name.
7. I dedicate this business (mention the name) to the Lord, in the name of Jesus Christ.
8. Every person of power that will want to rise against the success of this business, oh Lord hinder them in Jesus name.

9. All that is required for the success of this business, heaven release it in Jesus name.

10. We command growth, increase, progress, success and profit into this business/organization in the name of Jesus.

11. This business will not die, it will not fail, it will prosper on a daily basis in the name of Jesus.

12. I pour upon you (business) this anointing, and zeal up this declaration upon you in the name of Jesus. (anoint any material representing the business, and anoint the business environment in the name of Jesus).

It is not only a new business you dedicate. You can dedicate or rededicate that business/organization afresh. It will connect the business to divine source of blessing and things will begin to work.

CHAPTER 11

PRAYER FOR GLOBAL OPEN HEAVENS

The LORD shall open unto thee his good treasure, the heaven to give the rain unto thy land in his season, and to bless all the work of thine hand: and thou shalt lend unto many nations, and thou shalt not borrow. Deut 28:12

When the heavens of your blessing opens the blessing of God will pour upon it and you be so much blessed that you will never borrow or be in debt, but rather you will be giving out to nations. Some business heavens open on the very first day, and people begin to flood into it for patronage. Why many businesses never experience instant open heaven until many days, month, years afterward, that is why you need to open the heavens with your prayers.

Have you ever in your life commanded the morning, or made the dawn know its place, Job 38:12 (Net Bible)

This scripture connote that you are responsible to command your heavens to open, not only your heaven, you are to command how you want the day to favor your business. When the heaven of a business opens, it will enjoy customers, sales, profit and increase on a daily basis. Don't just pray for the heaven to open but to remain opened. The cloud can gather dews enough to make a rain, it is when the cloud opens up that the shower begins.

There are different dimension of open heavens. Some business experience dew like blessing, some enjoys shower of blessing. It is not the size of a business that determines the measure of open heaven, but the size of your authority and faith.

What open heaven does to the business?

- Open heaven makes the business enjoy divine backing.
- Open heaven make the blessings of heaven rain upon the business. Deut. 28:12
- It commands angelic traffic. Gen. 28:10-17.
- It opens doors of connection to the business.
- It keeps the eyes of the Lord upon the business day and night.
- It makes revelation and the word of the Lord available per time to know what the business has to do to scale through all challenges and then move on to succeed. Ezek.1:1

Scriptural verification:
If ye walk in my statutes, and keep my commandments, and do them; Then I will give you rain in due season, and the land shall yield her increase, and the trees of the field shall yield their fruit. Lev. 26:2-3

And he shall be like a tree planted by the rivers of water, that bringeth forth his fruit in his season; his leaf also shall not wither; and whatsoever he doeth shall prosper. Psalm 1:3

Blessed [is] the man that trusteth in the LORD, and whose hope the LORD is. For he shall be as a tree planted by the waters, and [that] spreadeth out her roots by the river, and shall not see when heat cometh, but her leaf shall be green; and shall not be careful in the year of drought, neither shall cease from yielding fruit. Jer. 17:7-8

There are different areas of open heaven. Heaven of sales, profit, customers, increase, growth, favor, resources, just name it. Whichever of this heaven is opened over a business is what the business will enjoy without limit.

Jesus commanded the wind and storm to cease and they obeyed. Everything in creation has an ear, and they all have the ability to obey the word of God in the name of Jesus, heavens don't open on its own, it is your spiritual responsibility to get the heaven to open for your business at your command.

Conditions for open heavens

1. Maintain a good relationship with God.
2. Don't play pranks with your workers and customers.
3. Be faithful in your tithing.
4. Be faithful in all your business transactions.
5. Pray for it and have faith it has opened.

Scriptural confession

Hear, O LORD, [when] I cry with my voice: have mercy also upon me, and answer me. [When thou saidst], Seek ye my face; my heart said unto thee, Thy face, LORD, will I seek. Ps. 27:7-8

Wherefore God also hath highly exalted him, and given him a name which is above every name: That at the name of Jesus every knee should bow, of [things] in heaven, and [things] in earth, and [things] under the earth; And [that] every tongue should confess that Jesus Christ [is] Lord, to the glory of God the Father. Phil. 2:9-11

Give ear, O ye heavens, and I will speak; and hear, O earth, the words of my mouth.

Prayers

1. Oh yea heavens hear the word of the Lord, I command you in the name of Jesus to open and favor my business.
2. Heaven of this business breakthrough, open in the name of Jesus.
3. Heaven of this business helpers and customers open in the name of Jesus.
4. Every power in the heavenlies that want to stand as a barrier to the open heaven of this business be evacuated by fire in the name of Jesus.
5. Every power over this business terrain that has covered the heaven of this business, fall down and die in the name of Jesus.
6. Every cloud of darkness, obstacle in the heavenly against this business be removed in the name of Jesus.
7. Heavens of continuous sales and blessings open over this business in the name of Jesus.
8. Heaven of new innovation, ideas and resources be opened over this business in the name of Jesus.
9. Rain of favor fall upon this business in the name of Jesus.
10. I decree this business will not experience a closed heaven but perpetual open heavens in Jesus name.

11. Any mistake and error, sins and iniquity that want to stand as an obstacle to the open heaven of this business, be nullified by the blood of Jesus.
12. Heavens of continuous revelations and vision of what to do per time to expand and increase be opened in Jesus name.
13. (mention the business name) You will do well in the name of Jesus.

PRAYER OF SANCTIFICATION

And Moses took the anointing oil, and anointed the tabernacle and all that [was] therein, and sanctified them. Lev 8:10

Sanctification means to cleanse the business from physical and spiritual pollution. Jesus entered into the temple and sent out those who are buying and selling. And said, my house shall be called a house of prayer not a house of merchandise.

And the Jews' passover was at hand, and Jesus went up to Jerusalem, And found in the temple those that sold oxen and sheep and doves, and the changers of money sitting: And when he had made a scourge of small cords, he drove them all out of the temple, and the sheep, and the oxen; and poured out the changers' money, and overthrew the tables. And said unto them that sold doves, Take these things hence; make not my Father's house an house of merchandise. John 2:13-16

When a place is sanctified it will be made fit for habitation physically and spiritually. We all want to live in a Rehoboth, a place of rest. Likewise we want to do business in a place where there will be not difficulties and obstruction to the progress of the business, but rather a place suitable and comfortable for the business and all the work force. Sanctification is therefore needed for this reason. Anywhere you want to settle your business you must make sure the place is spiritually palatable, just as you would want it to be, physically. A surrounding that is dirty and polluted in the realm of the spirit will be stinking to people in the physical. You may not be able to smell it but people can smell things. Save guide the interest of your business and vicinity from pollution that can make the sales to drag and customer to feel uneasy with transacting with you as a result of the spiritual nature of the environment.

Purpose For Sanctification

1. To cleanse the land from any curses and it effect.
2. To cleanse the land of any charms that might have been buried on it and it negative effect on the location and the business.
3. To cleanse the land of bloodshed, peradventure someone's blood has ever been shed on that land.
4. To cleanse the land of every spiritual pollution.
5. To terminate and clear off any evil altar and there operation over the land by the precious blood of Jesus.

Instruction

Get your anointing oil ready before prayer; Anoint the business premises, anoint every offices, anoint the equipments all in the name of Jesus.

Scripture confession

And now also the axe is laid unto the root of the trees: therefore every tree which bringeth not forth good fruit is hewn down, and cast into the fire. Matt 3:10

But he answered and said, Every plant, which my heavenly Father hath not planted, shall be rooted up. Matt 15:13

Prayers

1. I uproot anything God has not planted into this land, building in the name of Jesus.
2. Every altar in this land and building be destroyed by the blood of Jesus.
3. Every altar in this land and building be consumed by fire in Jesus name.
4. Every demonic spirit on this land and inside this building I send you out in the name of Jesus.
5. Any agreement and covenant binding any strange spirits to this land, I break it by the blood of Jesus today.
6. I break every yoke, evil covenant and evil order operating on this land and building in the name of Jesus.
7. Anything that has been buried in this land, be uprooted and destroyed by fire in the name of Jesus.
8. Any caldron in this land, catch fire in the name of Jesus.
9. Any curse over this land and building, be cancelled by the blood of Jesus.
10. I redeem this land and building back with the blood of Jesus.
11. Every spiritual pollution in this land and building be neutralize by the blood of Jesus.
12. Every evil burial ground swallowing the glory and fortune of people in this building and land, catch fire, be destroyed by fire in the name of Jesus.
13. Get your anointing oil, begin to anoint every corner of that land, office space and building, with the anointing, declaring, I anoint this premises with the blood of Jesus. I take charge of this land and building physically and spiritually in the name of Jesus.

14. I declared this land sanctified by the blood of Jesus in the name of Jesus.
15. By the authority in the name of Jesus I declared this place suitable for business in the name of Jesus.
16. Thank you Jesus for the cleansing of this place, let your glory fill this place in the name of Jesus.

13

PRAYER FOR FLOW
OF CUSTOMER AND SALES

Jesus said,
No man can come to me, except the Father which hath sent me draw him: and I will raise him up at the last day. John 6:44

Come ye near unto me, hear ye this; I have not spoken in secret from the beginning; from the time that it was, there [am] I: and now the Lord GOD, and his Spirit, hath sent me. Thus saith the LORD, thy Redeemer, the Holy One of Israel; **I [am] the LORD thy God which teacheth thee to profit,** *which leadeth thee by the way [that] thou shouldest go. Isaiah 48:16-17.*

It is God that draws people to things, and things to people. When you involve God to bring customers that is called divine awareness, the product begins to receive acceptance.

When God draws people to your product and services, it will enjoy uncommon sales. Product and services may be good and even be the best in the market place. People may admire it, like it, and even speak about it, yet they may not patronize it. They may even need it and they will leave and go and patronize another product not as good as yours. But when God breathe upon a product, even if it is not the best, they will just prefer it for one reason or the other.

No company really knows what works; it is God that makes things to work. It is not what people really want that sells, it is what God has blessed.

Scriptural confession
For wheresoever's the carcass is, there will the eagles be gathered together. Matt 24:28

Prayer
1. Oh Lord breath upon our products and services and make it enjoy patronage in Jesus name.
2. Oh Lord, draw the attention of people to this organization/product and services in Jesus name.
3. Oh Lord, open the eyes of people to this organization/product/services and make them buy into it in Jesus name.
4. Oh Lord, bring us the right staff that will have the zeal for the success of this organization in Jesus name.
5. Oh Lord, let our product and services appeal to our customers in Jesus name.
6. Oh Lord, Flood this business with continuous flow of profitable customer in Jesus name.
7. Any customer that will bring bad name to this business, Holy Spirit send them away before they do in Jesus name.
8. Let the door be open for sales and customer in this business in Jesus name.
9. Let the interest of people be drawn to this organization/business in Jesus name.

10. Help us to improve and meet up to the thirst and demand of our customers in Jesus name.

11. Every power in this environment that use to turn customers to enemy, you will not succeed over this business in Jesus name.

12. Oh Lord, let your grace rest upon our product and services in Jesus name.

13. The anointing that will turn our customers to our marketers/partners fall upon this business in Jesus name.

14. Any spirit from anywhere that want to discourage our customers and people against this business, you will not prosper in Jesus name.

15. I arrest the operation of any environmental and territorial powers in Jesus name.

16. Any bad mouthed customer that may want to stop the flow of sales and acceptance of our product and services through negative utterance be silenced in Jesus name.

17. Oh Lord, empower this organization and all the staff to meet up to the demands of our customers in Jesus name.

18. Let our products and services become delights to our customers in Jesus name.

19. By the authority in Jesus name, my business/organization will enjoy daily rise in customers and sales in Jesus name.

20. I command in Jesus name, as the products increases, the customer will increase in Jesus name.

21. I decree in Jesus name, no product will be out of date before the sales in Jesus name.

22. I decree in Jesus name, there will be no wastage of material, resources or product in this business in Jesus name.
23. Every yoke of limitation in sales, break in Jesus name.
24. Every yoke of limited customers, break in Jesus name.
25. I decree upon this business/organization/products unlimited patronage in the name of Jesus.
26. I reject creditors in the name of Jesus.
27. Anointing for uncommon flow of sales and customers fall upon this business.
28. Anywhere this company/organization/product get to, hear the word of the Lord, you will enjoy unlimited favor and patronage in Jesus name.
29. I abort and cancel every agenda of promise and fail over this business in Jesus name.
30. Any power assigned to hinder customer and sales of our goods and services, I rebuke you in Jesus name.
31. Every strongman of darkness, monitoring this business sales and customers, be arrested by the net of fire in Jesus name.
32. Every loophole the enemy may capitalize on to cause setback for this business, I cover it with the blood of Jesus.
33. Any product or mistake that will dent the image of this business be aborted in Jesus name.
34. Every mistake and error that can damage the integrity of this business, be destroy before it ever manifest in Jesus name.

CHAPTER 14

PRAYER FOR MANIFESTATION
OF BUSINESS GLORY

This beginning of miracles did Jesus in Cana of Galilee, and manifested forth his glory; and his disciples believed on him. John 2:11.

Everything in creation has a glory, and so every business has it own glory. The glory is what makes the business to be recognized and prosper. A glory is like the engine of a business. An active glory is like a catalyst to the success of a business. Like the seed of a plant, like the key to a lock. If the glory is dormant the business will be dormant. The business will be crawling when it should be flying.

Every glory has the potential to manifest. The glory of a business is the virtue in that business that makes the business to sky rocket in sales; it also makes the business to shine. When the glory is missing in action failure will be evident.

Many businesses are not prospering because her glory has been covered, until the glory is revealed people will not see the potential of the business. The glory brings divine attention to the business.

Why you need to pray for the glory?

1. The glory can be hindered from manifesting.
2. The glory can be covered.
3. The glory can be hijacked.
4. The glory can be sleeping.
5. The glory may need activation to function

Scriptural confessions

But thou, O LORD, shalt endure for ever; and thy remembrance unto all generations. Thou shalt arise, [and] have mercy upon Zion: for the time to favour her, yea, the set time, is come. For thy servants take pleasure in her stones, and favour the dust thereof. So the heathen shall fear the name of the LORD, and all the kings of the earth thy glory. When the LORD shall build up Zion(put your business name), he shall appear in his glory. He will regard the prayer of the destitute, and not despise their prayer. Psalm 102:12-17

1. My business glory hear the word of the Lord, it is written, I will decree a thing and it shall be established, I command you to be activated to function in the name of Jesus.
2. The glory of my business, be quickened by the Spirit of the Lord in the name of Jesus.
3. Every evil covering over the glory of my business be removed in the name of Jesus.
4. Any attack against the manifestation of my business glory, expire in the name of Jesus.
5. My glory, my business glory wherever you are in hiding, by the power in the name of Jesus, appear and manifest.
6. My business glory arise and shine in the name of Jesus.

7. Anointing for revival, fall upon my business glory in the name of Jesus.

8. Any cage where my business glory may be caged, scatter by fire in the name of Jesus.

9. Any where my business glory has been kept in hiding, Holy Ghost fire locate the place and consume the place, and set the glory free in Jesus name.

10. Angels of God ordained for deliverance, locate my glory wherever it is, and deliver it in the name of Jesus.

11. My business glory manifest by fire in the name of Jesus.

CHAPTER 15

PRAYER FOR DIVINE CONNECTION

Divine connection is the art of God bringing one that needs help to one who can help him. It is the coming in contact of two people that will be of mutual benefit to each other or one person being a blessing to the other, by the divine arrangement of God.

And the word of the LORD came unto him, saying, Arise, get thee to Zarephath, which [belongeth] to Zidon, and dwell there: behold, I have commanded a widow woman there to sustain thee. So he arose and went to Zarephath. And when he came to the gate of the city, behold, the widow woman [was] there gathering of sticks: and he called to her, and said, Fetch me, I pray thee, a little water in a vessel, that I may drink. And as she was going to fetch [it], he called to her, and said, Bring me, I pray thee, a morsel of bread in thine hand. And she said, [As] the LORD thy God liveth, I have not a cake, but an handful of meal in a barrel, and a little oil in a cruse: and, behold, I [am] gathering two sticks, that I may go in and dress it for me and my son, that we may eat it, and die. And Elijah said unto her, Fear not; go [and] do as thou hast said: but make me thereof a little cake first, and bring [it] unto me, and after make for thee and for thy son. For thus saith the LORD God of Israel, The barrel of meal shall not waste, neither shall the cruse of oil fail, until the day [that] the LORD sendeth rain upon the earth. And she went and did according to the saying of Elijah: and she, and he, and her house, did eat [many] days. [And] the barrel of meal wasted not, neither did the cruise of oil fail, according to the word of the LORD, which he spake by Elijah.

Divine means supernatural. Divine connection is the involvement of God in bringing two things together. Some business will never experience success until they are connected to right business partners, organization, people that will take it to the next level. Divine connection brings advancement, progress and resources. Some organization and business need divine connection to right people or right market, for them to experience major breakthrough. Some need divine connection to right ideas and innovation. Some need to be connected to the right places and location. Some need to be connected to the right organizations. Some need to be connected to the right resources. Divine connection opens a business to the right opportunity. This is a common thing with God. God knows how to connect His children's business and bring them to a new order of breakthrough.

BENEFIT OF DIVINE CONNECTION
1. It connects you to the right people.
2. It connects you to good resources.
3. It connects you to sponsors and investors.
4. It moves you to the next phase of your plans.

Scriptural confession
The steps of a [good] man are ordered by the LORD: and he delighteth in his way. Ps 37:23
For the Lord GOD will help me; therefore shall I not be confounded: therefore have I set my face like a flint, and I know that I shall not be ashamed. Isa 50:7

Prayers for divine connection

1. Oh Lord, my father, open the door of divine connection to me, locally and internationally in Jesus name.

2. Oh Lord, connect me to those who matter to my lifting and breakthrough in the name of Jesus.

3. Oh Lord, connect me to my destiny helpers in the name of Jesus.

4. Every power blocking my access to my helpers, be destroyed in the name of Jesus

5. Every barrier between me and my opportunities be removed in the name of Jesus.

6. Every distance between me and my helpers be bridged by the Spirit of God in the name of Jesus.

7. Every embargo that kept me stagnant be removed in the name of Jesus.

8. Anywhere this business has been caged, oh Lord, release her and let her be seen in Jesus name.

9. Whatever has covered this business, be removed in the name of Jesus.

10. Any power that is stopping this business from moving forward, enough is enough, release her and die in Jesus name.

11. Heaven of divine connection, open unto this business in the name of Jesus.

12. Divine favor of God that brings the right connection, rest upon this business in the name of Jesus.

CHAPTER 16

PRAYER AGAINST
FORCES OF HINDRANCE

But we, brethren, being taken from you for a short time in presence, not in heart, endeavoured the more abundantly to see your face with great desire. Wherefore we would have come unto you, even I Paul, once and again; but Satan hindered us. 1Thess 2:17-18.

A force is any power that opposes or support the movement of any object. A force of hindrance is that force behind hindrance. This force hinders progress, testimony, expectation and meaningful vision. When this force is at work, it makes progress impossible. A force of hindrance is a spiritual force that has been demonically programmed to cause a painful setback for a business and her progress.

This force is a spirit of darkness from the pit of hell that specializes in hindering good things. It is a monitoring agent, that monitors every channel good things can be coming from, and will strategically position itself to block it. They cause frustrating hindrance and unexplainable delay to expectation.

When a force of hindrance is at work, it will not allow the business to meet it targeted sales, progress, demand and expectation. What has been projected for the business to achieve within a certain period will be impossible. These spirits of hindrance causes a big time disappointment to the business people. It will totally hinder good things from locating the business and the business owners inclusive. Repeated hindrance of good flow of resources into a business will end the business in bankruptcy.

Negative Influence Of Hindrance

1. Hindrance will cause stagnation.
2. Hindrance will cause maximum stoppage of sales and patronage.
3. Hindrance will not allow the money invested to be regained at the right time.
4. Hindrance will make the business waste money on advertisement without response from targeted customers.
5. Hindrance will leave you asking question like, what are we suppose to do that we have not done, what is lacking, why is there no envisaged progress? However, know that the force of hindrance is arrested by the operation of the force of prayer.

How to overcome the force of address

1. Be willing to address it.
2. Fast and pray with a roaring authority in Jesus name.

Scriptures to address

Wherefore God also hath highly exalted him, and given him a name which is above every name: That at the name of Jesus every knee should bow, of [things] in heaven, and [things] in earth, and [things] under the earth; And [that] every tongue should confess that Jesus Christ [is] Lord, to the glory of God the Father. Phil. 2:9-11

Verily I say unto you, Whatsoever ye shall bind on earth shall be bound in heaven: and whatsoever ye shall loose on earth shall be loosed in heaven. Matt 18:18.

1. Oh Lord, release upon me fresh fire in the name of Jesus.
2. Oh Lord, be willing to deliver my business from every negative force operating against her today in Jesus name.
3. Every spirit of hindrance, assigned to monitor my opportunity and expectation I stop you in the name of Jesus.
4. Every spirit of hindrance, assigned to frustrate me, I bind you in the name of Jesus.
5. Every spirit, giving information about me and diverting good things from locating my life, I bind you in the name of Jesus.
6. Every spiritual blockage, blocking good things in my business, be removed in the name of Jesus.
7. Every weapon of hindrance employed against my life and business, catch fire in the name of Jesus.
8. Every Satanic strategy the enemy is engaging against my business, scatter in the name of Jesus.
9. I reject every operation of hindering spirit in the name of Jesus.
10. I declare that in the name of Jesus, the way is cleared and opened for easy flow of operation in the name of Jesus.

CHAPTER 17

PRAYER AGAINST
TERRITORIAL FORCES

Then lifted I up mine eyes, and saw, and behold four horns. And I said unto the angel that talked with me, What [be] these? And he answered me, These [are] the horns which have scattered Judah, Israel, and Jerusalem. And the LORD shewed me four carpenters. Then said I, What come these to do? And he spake, saying, These [are] the horns which have scattered Judah, so that no man did lift up his head: but these are come to fray them, to cast out the horns of the Gentiles, which lifted up [their] horn over the land of Judah to scatter it. Zech 1:18-21

A horn is a demonic power that put people under suffering and captivity. There are horns of darkness over the territory of Judah, Israel and Jerusalem that keeps the people under oppression and does not allow them to lift up their heads. Horns of the gentiles are the weapons of the powers of darkness in operation over a territory to cause hardship, setback and frustration, this amount to territorial forces.

Territorial forces are one of the most terrifying forces that operate in some business environment to hinder the growth and progress of the business. They are principalities and powers that rule over the activities of operation in the community. These are the powers that close the heaven over a territory, and determine what comes in and what goes out. They tie people down to one position, cause loses and reduction in the welfare of people.

How To Deal With Them

1. Fast and pray for 3days, or more.
2. Pray violent prayer, in the arena of your business office at midnight
3. Pray in team. Get someone to join you, if no one, then you can do it alone. For one will chase a thousand and two will chase ten thousand the scriptures says.

Scriptural confession:

(For the weapons of our warfare [are] not carnal, but mighty through God to the pulling down of strong holds;) Casting down imaginations, and every high thing that exalteth itself against the knowledge of God, and bringing into captivity every thought to the obedience of Christ; 2Cor 10:4-5.

And the God of peace shall bruise Satan under your feet shortly. The grace of our Lord Jesus Christ [be] with you. Amen. Rom 16:20

And the angels which kept not their first estate, but left their own habitation, he hath reserved in everlasting chains under darkness unto the judgment of the great day. Jude 1:6

And I heard a loud voice saying in heaven, Now is come salvation, and strength, and the kingdom of our God, and the power of his Christ: for the accuser of our brethren is cast down, which accused them before our God day and night.

And they overcame him by the blood of the Lamb, and by the word of their testimony; and they loved not their lives unto the death. Rev 12:10-11

Behold, I [am] against thee, O destroying mountain, saith the LORD, which destroyest all the earth: and I will stretch out mine hand upon thee, and roll thee down from the rocks, and will make thee a burnt mountain. Jer. 51:25

Prayers

1. Altars of territorial power, catch fire in the name of Jesus.

2. Altars of environmental power, scatter by the fire of the Holy Ghost in the name of Jesus.

3. Every stronghold of darkness around this business arena that can hinder and affect my business, scatter by fire in the name of Jesus.

4. Every territorial forces ruling over this terrain, enough of your operation, park your load and get out of this vicinity in the name of Jesus.

5. It is written, light shines in darkness and darkness cannot comprehend, I command all territorial forces militating against this business to be arrested by the fire of the Holy Spirit in the name of Jesus.

6. I command the fire of God to saturate this environment in the name of Jesus.

7. Every covenant that establish you in this territory, I destroy it by the blood of Jesus in the name of Jesus.

8. Every sacrifice that has been rendered and use to be rendered in this territory I cancel it in the name of Jesus.

9. The earth is the Lords' and the fullness therefore, I therefore command you to vacate this terrain in the name of Jesus.

10. Every evil injunction that has tied you to this environment and territory, I cancel it in the name of Jesus.

11. Every operation of territorial forces over this territory expire in the name of Jesus.

12. Every road block, evil gate that has been mounted over this territory to stop good things, I command you be removed completely in the name of Jesus.
13. I invite the Holy Spirit to come and reign over this environment in the name of Jesus.
14. Every evil meeting point in this arena, I scatter it in the name of Jesus.
15. I change every evil name that has been given this environment in the name of Jesus Christ. I call this place Rehoboth, Beulah in the name of Jesus Christ.
16. I establish the authority of Christ supremacy over this area in the name of Jesus Christ.
17. In this environment, no more loses, no more challenges, let the heavens of blessing of this place be opened day and night in the name of Jesus.

CHAPTER 18

PRAYER FOR THE RIGHT
WORKERS/STAFF

The steps of a [good] man are ordered by the LORD: and he delighteth in his way. Ps 37:23

Finding the right staff. Without exception, every business executive I speak to says that one of their biggest challenges is staff – finding the right staff, retaining them, and ensuring they buy into the vision of the business. I'll freely admit that I have no magic answers here. In fact, if someone could develop a formula for recruiting and engaging the right team members, they would make millions. A small business is almost like a family, and, like many families, they can work well, or they can be dysfunctional. In big companies, the human resource challenge is politics and fit in the workplace, but when it comes to small business, its personalities and skill. When you work in a small environment, each team member's personality can have a huge impact on the harmony and productivity of the business. Curled from Forbes online, contribution of Cheryl Conner.

People you chose to work with determines how thing is working in your business. You can choose people yourself, and God can lead the right people to your organization without much stress. Right workers will do the business much good.

Every organization has team of staff operating in different department and performing different key role to achieve the goal of the organization. If you don't rightly select your staffs, there will be loophole in the business; loophole is open doors for the enemy to perpetuate wickedness and to cause havoc for the business. etc, which will cost the business lot of loses. To cut this cost you need the help of God in directing those right people to you. The wrong staff will mess up your dream. Choose with insight and divine direction.

Benefits Of Right Workers

1. They will be committed.
2. They will love the business.
3. They will handle it like their own.
4. They will be loyal.
5. They will be reliable.
6. They will work for the growth and progress of the business.
7. They will give necessary boost to the success of the business.
8. They will stand by you in good and bad times.
9. They are your business success team.

Scriptural confession:
Calling a ravenous bird from the east, the man that executeth my counsel from a far country: yea, I have spoken [it], I will also bring it to pass; I have purposed [it], I will also do it. Isa 46:11
The steps of a [good] man are ordered by the LORD: and he delighteth in his way. Ps 37:23

Prayers
1. Oh Lord, send me workers like angels in Jesus name.

2. Oh Lord, order the steps of everyone you have ordained to work with me in this business, department, organization, ministry to me in Jesus name.

3. I abort every evil trick of the devil to manipulate wrong people to this business in Jesus name.

4. Anything in my life, attracting the wrong people, be destroyed in Jesus name.

5. Any power attracting wrong people to me, I bind you and I stop your operations in the name of Jesus.

6. I reject wrong workers in the name of Jesus.

7. Anointing for good staff, fall upon this business in the name of Jesus.

8. Any functional curse in my life, in this environment, in this line of business that draws in wrong people be broken in the name of Jesus.

9. I reject every form of spiritual blindfolding and confusion in selection of workers in the name of Jesus.

10. I reject manipulation of evil voice in the selection of right workers in the name of Jesus.

11. I come against powers from hell that wants to run down this business in the name of Jesus.

12. I shut the door against the wrong workers and open doors for the right staff to locate this business in the name of Jesus.

13. Every evil veil over this business I tear you off in the name of Jesus.

14. I command blessed and destined people into this business in the name of Jesus.

15. I will not be the wrong person in this business in Jesus name.

16. God will not reject my work in Jesus name.

CHAPTER 19

PRAYER FOR SUCCESS SECRET
OF THE BUSINESS

The secret [things belong] unto the LORD our God: but those [things which are] revealed [belong] unto us and to our children for ever, that [we] may do all the words of this law. Deut 29:29

Every business has a secret, and it is in the secret of that business that you will find the business success code. God is the God of secrets and revelation. God reveals deep and secret things. No man can know what he has not been taught, shown or experience. It is only God that knows all things, because he made them all. However, it is what God reveals that is a secrets.

When God reveals the secret of the success of a business to you, it will help you to know what you should do and shouldn't do. It will make you to escape where others are trapped, and make you know what to do to succeed where others a failing.

The success of Daniel is based on the fact that God revealed to him the secret that no one knows about the dream of the king. God revealed to him the dream and interpretation of the dream of King Nebuchadnezzar. Dan. 2.28. The king dreamt and forgot his dream. It took the revelation of this dream by God to make Daniel to succeed where others has failed. God is a revealer of deep and secret things. In secret there are answers and secret is always a eye opener.

Then was the secret revealed unto Daniel in a night vision. Then Daniel blessed the God of heaven. Dan 2:19

He revealeth the deep and secret things: he knoweth what [is] in the darkness, and the light dwelleth with him. Dan 2:22

The secret you have access to will determine the speed of your success and the measure of your breakthrough in the business. When God shows you the secret, it is to help you to get ahead of those who have been there before you. God will not show you a secret that will not better your situation. Be desirous to see what God needs to show you to succeed in that business. Every business has a key. However, some business has different keys that will work in the hands of different individuals. That means the key that works in the hand of Mr. Alex, may not be the key that will work in the hand of Mr Jack and so on. It is important to have direct access to your own business success secret.

Benefits of this

1. It will save you from running into loses.
2. It will save you from trial and errors.
3. It will make you know where to channel your energy.
4. It will make you to make it in the business fast.
5. It will give you an edge over those who have been before you.
6. It will put into your hand the keys to succeed in that business for life.

Scriptures

Thus saith the LORD the maker thereof, the LORD that formed it, to establish it; the LORD [is] his name; Call unto me, and I will answer thee, and shew thee great and mighty things, which thou knowest not. Jer 33:2-3

Thus saith the LORD, thy Redeemer, the Holy One of Israel; I [am] the LORD thy God which teacheth thee to profit, which leadeth thee by the way [that] thou shouldest go. Isa 48:17

Trust in the LORD with all thine heart; and lean not unto thine own understanding. In all thy ways acknowledge him, and he shall direct thy paths. Prov 3:5-6

Prayers

1. Oh Lord, by your mercy answer me today and show me things.
2. Oh Lord, rend the heavens open and show me all about this business in Jesus name.
3. I will not miss my moment of visitation and revelation in Jesus name.
4. Oh Lord, show me the secret of success of this business in Jesus name.
5. Oh Lord, release upon me the gift and the grace I need to see what you want to show me in Jesus name.
6. Oh Lord, let what you show me result to outstanding success of this business in Jesus name.
7. Oh Lord, teach me how to profit maximally in this business in Jesus name.

STAGE THREE

PRAYER FOR BUSINESSES AT ALL STAGES

Any business can bankrupt at any stage if right measures are not put in place. Business liquidate when is not able to meet up with his vision and mission again. A business can close down, or bought over by other successful business. If you don't want to ground that business, engage this scripture. The business of Isaac blessed more than ten generation.
Genesis 26: 18-22, and John 4:6-12

CHAPTER 20

PRAYER OF CLEANSING OF
OFFICES AND FACTORIES

And thou shalt offer every day a bullock [for] a sin offering for atonement: and thou shalt cleanse the altar, when thou hast made atonement for it, and thou shalt anoint it, to sanctify it. Exod. 29:36

Every year your business, offices, factories has to be cleansed. Many business are in an accursed land, many has been invaded by strange spirit of loses, failure, difficulty and hardship and so on.

When these spirits are at work, they will frustrate the business based on their evil tags and operation. If spirit of loses enter into an office or a business outlet, they will begin to experience loses. Some are spirit of hardship. As you are making effort to make things work, some powers are making it more difficult. They have to be arrested and the environment has to be recaptured again in the name of the Lord.

When a strongman armed keepeth his palace, his goods are in peace. But when a stronger than he shall come upon him, and overcome him, he taketh from him all his armour wherein he trusted and divideth his spoil. Luke 11:21-22

To cleanse means to send out the strong man operating in your business terrain, and putting an end to all their operations.

Before you can carry out this exercise, you must be sanctified. It is the spirit that confirms our word. When you leave in sin or you are not yet saved(Given your life to Jesus Christ) and you try this, you are putting yourself in danger. Follow the salvation process and give your life to Jesus that is your security against attacks. Jesus is described to be the head of all principality and power. Col. 2:10.

Tools for cleansing

- Anointing oil.
  Anointing oil means the presence of God. It destroys yokes and lift burden because it has become a virtue of power.
- Blood of sprinkling.
  The blood sanctifies the business environment from every physical and spiritual pollution.
- The word of God.
- Prayers.

Scriptures

And found in the temple those that sold oxen and sheep and doves, and the changers of money sitting: And when he had made a scourge of small cords, he drove them all out of the temple, and the sheep, and the oxen; and poured out the changers' money, and overthrew the tables; And said unto them that sold doves, Take these things hence; make not my Father's house an house of merchandise. John 2:14-16

I have pursued mine enemies, and overtaken them: neither did I turn again till they were consumed. I have wounded them that they were not able to rise: they are fallen under my feet. For thou hast girded me with strength unto the battle: thou hast subdued under me those that rose up against me. Thou hast also given me the necks of mine enemies; that I might destroy them that hate me. They cried, but [there was] none to save [them: even] unto the LORD, but he answered them not. Then did I beat them small as the dust before the wind: I did cast them out as the dirt in the streets. Thou hast delivered me from the strivings of the people; [and] thou hast made me the head of the heathen: a people [whom] I have not known shall serve me. As soon as they hear of me, they shall obey me: the strangers shall submit themselves unto me. The strangers shall fade away, and be afraid out of their close places. Psalm 18:37-45

Prayers

1. Holy Spirit of God, I usher you in to take over this place in the name of Jesus.
2. I plead the blood of Jesus in this environment and over this place in the name of Jesus
3. Every stranger in this environment, your end has come pack your load and go out and never come back in the name of Jesus.
4. I take over this business terrain in the name of Jesus Christ.
5. I deliver this business and this land from every forces of darkness in the name of Jesus Christ.
6. Every habitation of darkness in this business terrain, scatter in the name of Jesus.
7. Every altar of darkness in this environment waging war against this business, collapse and be destroyed by the fire of the Holy Ghost in the name of Jesus.

8. I sprinkle the blood of Jesus over every evil sacrifice, evil works done in this terrain and I command you to become powerless and destroyed in the name of Jesus.

9. Fire of God, fall over this environment and barricade this business from strangers in the name of Jesus.

10. Let the heavens be open for the angels of favor and breakthrough to locate this business.

11. I command divine turn around for this business and all the staffs in the name of Jesus.

12. Every dark cloud and covering over this business be removed in the name of Jesus.

13. Every blockage and hindrances stopping good things from locating this business be removed now in the name of Jesus.

14. Holy Ghost and fire fill this business arena in the name of Jesus.

Engage The Anointing and Declare this:

Every curse on the ground, as the anointing touches the ground, be destroyed in the name of Jesus.

Every evil feet, evil dust, spell on this ground be destroyed in the name of Jesus.

Every evil forest in this ground be consumed by fire of the Holy Ghost.

Every throne of darkness on this ground I overthrow you in the name of Jesus and I command you to be consumed by fire in the name of Jesus.

Every invisible altar on this ground be destroyed by the fire of the Holy Ghost in the name of Jesus.

CHAPTER 21

ENEMIES OF MY VISION, BE ARRESTED

Where [there is] no vision, the people perish: but he that keepeth the law, happy [is] he. Prov 29:18.

Your vision is your business and your business is your vision. If you lack vision, you lack business. You must guide your vision with total determination. Not everyone that has vision can successfully turn it to a business. Many great visions never get to materialize because of several internal and external forces waging war against the vision. *Your vision is your business.*

Every great vision has great friends and great enemies. *There is no vision without believers (Those who buy into the vision) and there is no vision also without enemies (Those who want it to die).* The believers of your vision are the people that will support you and go extra mile just for you to achieve your vision. These believers are willing to contribute their time, resources and idea to bring the vision into existence. While the enemies of your vision are the forces and people that want to destroy, frustrate and hinder the manifestation of your vision. The passion you have for your vision determines the security you give to your vision. Your vision needs security. The security will protect it from every enemy and help you to materialize.

Benefit Of Protecting Your Vision

- Your vision is your destination.
- Your vision is your future.
- Your vision is your business.
- Your vision is your asset.
- Your vision is the solution to your present predicament.
- Your vision is your throne of glory.
- Your vision is your key to life of fulfillment.
- Your vision is your money.

ENEMIES OF VISION
Internal enemies
Fear

Low self esteem

Negative attitude

Giving up too soon

Procrastination

Bad Habit

Laziness

External Enemies
Wrong association

Curse

Faulty Foundation

Satanic attacks

Wrong location etc

How To Protect Your Vision

1. Avoid telling your vision to those who envy you.
2. Avoid telling your vision to those with evil intention.

3. Avoid telling your vision to those who don't want good things.
4. Avoid telling your vision to those who love to steal vision.
5. Guide your vision by wisdom.
6. Pray for your vision.
7. Share your vision with only those who believe in it.
8. Be willing and determine to pursue your vision.
9. Don't give your vision to those who don't have passion to run it.

Scriptural confession

To subvert a man in his cause, the Lord approveth not. Who [is] he [that] saith, and it cometh to pass, [when] the Lord commandeth [it] not? Lam 3:36-37

I know that, whatsoever God doeth, it shall be forever: nothing can be put to it, nor any thing taken from it: and God doeth [it], that [men] should fear before him. Eccl 3:14.

Prayers

1. Oh Lord thank you for this vision.
2. My vision will not die in Jesus name.
3. Every force that wants to stop my vision from manifesting be arrested by fire in Jesus name.
4. Every strongman assigned against my vision, I disconnect you by fire in the name of Jesus.
5. Any curse issued to silence my vision, be cancelled in the name of Jesus.
6. Every evil arrow fired against my vision backfire and die in the name of Jesus.

7. Any close enemy monitoring my vision to kill it, you will not prosper in the name of Jesus.

8. Anointing to fulfill my vision come upon me in Jesus name.

9. Power of God to succeed fall upon my vision in the name of Jesus.

10. Every battle in my life fighting my vision die by fire.

11. Every negative forces around my life fighting my vision die by fire in the name of Jesus.

12. Every agent of darkness assigned against my vision scatter by fire in the name of Jesus.

13. Holy Ghost fire locate all hindrance and obstacles to the fulfillment of my vision and consume it in the name of Jesus.

14. Helpers of my vision find your way to my vision in the name of Jesus.

15. Oh Lord, let the door of resources to actualize this vision be opened in the name of Jesus.

16. You my vision receive the power to move to the next level in the name of Jesus.

17. Oh Lord, let the eyes of those who are ordained to make this vision a success open to it in the name of Jesus.

18. I receive the grace and the wisdom to make this vision great in the name of Jesus.

CHAPTER 22

PRAYER FOR NEW CONTRACTS
AND OPPORTUNITIES

Therefore thy gates shall be open continually; they shall not be shut day nor night; that [men] may bring unto thee the forces of the Gentiles, and [that] their kings [may be] brought. Isa 60:11

If your company's operation is based on contract you need to pray. When the door of contract is open to your organization, you will be receiving contract so much that you will be rejecting some. However, if you are not receiving contract as supposed, then there is need for divine intervention. Intervention comes in when innovation is not working and your connections are not producing positive result.

If want to flourish all season in your organization you need to understand the efficacy of prayer in the time of drought. God turns things around through prayer of faith.

To get a contract to do, you don't need to lobby, you only need to sow. Sow the seed of prayer, sow the seed of fasting and sow the seed of money. All your seed put together open doors to contract and move the heart of relevant organization and government to open their doors of contract to you.

Scriptures to confess

Remember ye not the former things, neither consider the things of old. Behold, I will do a new thing; now it shall spring forth; shall ye not know it? I will even make a way in the wilderness, [and] rivers in the desert. The beast of the field shall honour me, the dragons and the owls: because I give waters in the wilderness, [and] rivers in the desert, to give drink to my people, my chosen. This people have I formed for myself; they shall shew forth my praise. Isa 43:18-21

Prayers

1. Oh Lord, favor our company in Jesus name.
2. Oh Lord, any mistake and error that has shut up our opportunities this past weeks, months, years pardon us and reverse it in Jesus name.
3. Oh Lord, cause our client to remember us for good in Jesus name.
4. Oh Lord, open doors of new contract for our organization in Jesus name.
5. Oh Lord, open the heavens of continuous flow of contracts for us in Jesus name.
6. Oh Lord, put an end to every drought and dryness in this organization in Jesus name
7. Every curse of rise and fall in this business be destroyed by the blood of Jesus.
8. Anointing to remove the yoke of joblessness be released upon this business in Jesus name.
9. Every doors shut up against the flow of contract be opened by the authority in Jesus name.
10. Any agent of hindrance against our operation be uprooted in Jesus name.

11. Every work of manipulation going on against our contract appointment be aborted in the name of Jesus.
12. Oh Lord, make our company the first choice of every company to partner with in Jesus name.
13. Oh Lord, give us the capacity to deliver as expected of us in Jesus name.
14. Thank you Lord Jesus.

CHAPTER 23

OH LORD, REVIVE THIS BUSINESS

They that dwell under his shadow shall return; they shall revive [as] the corn, and grow as the vine: the scent thereof [shall be] as the wine of Lebanon. Hos. 14:7

When the revival power of God falls upon a business, what has not been working will begin to work. To revive means to bring back to life, to rescue, to raise from dead, to give hope again. When a business is going down instead of going up, it needs revival. If a business is dead, it needs to be revived. When the spirit of God dwells upon anything dead, it brings it back to life.

The word of God is the reviving force of God. He sent his word into Jacob and it lighted upon Israel. When the word of God is spoken into a dead business, the word carries life and spirit. Life replaces whatever has been dead and brings it alive, while the spirit quickens things to operate and function as it is supposed.

He sent his word, and he delivers them and heals them. The word delivers them from destruction. It will deliver that business from that difficulty, and heal that business.

Through this prayer, God is going to revive your business in Jesus name.

Instruction

- **Check the foundation of the business**

  Do business check up and see where the problem begins. Ask questions and pray for the help of the Holy Spirit to help you make things right.

- **Pay the business tithe**

  That is your key to open heaven. Tithe is commanded, for heaven of blessing to be opened. Go ahead and pay, it. Give the tenth percentage of all your profit for that month first and go into prayers. Mal. 3:9-11.

- Wait on the Lord through fasting

Scriptural confession

Behold, God will not cast away a perfect [man], neither will he help the evil doers:
Till he fill thy mouth with laughing, and thy lips with rejoicing. Job 8: 21.

Prayer

1. Oh Lord, Visit this business in the name of Jesus.
2. Oh Lord, Bring back to life everything dead in this organization in Jesus name.
3. Whatever is killing this organization, reveal it now and remove it in Jesus name.
4. Deliver this organization from this condition and overturn the condition for the good of the organization.

5. Oh Lord, let there be a revival that will engineer uncommon breakthrough in this business in the mighty name of Jesus.

6. God, as you step into this business situation and bring it back to life, we will give you the glory and be faithful to you.

7. Anyone sabotaging this business, disgrace them oh Lord, in Jesus name.

8. Any evil seed in this business not allowing it to thrive be uprooted in Jesus name.

9. Anointing of the Holy Spirit for transformation and breakthrough fall upon this business in the name of Jesus.

10. Blood of Jesus flow to every source of this business to expose and flush out every obstacles and hindrances in the name of Jesus.

11. Oh Lord my father, let this business match up to her contemporaries in the name of Jesus.

12. I speak life into the realm of this business in the name of Jesus.

13. Anything programmed into this business to make it barren, unacceptable and dead backfire in Jesus name.

14. Thank you for answered prayers in the name of Jesus.

CHAPTER 24

PRAYER AGAINST CONTRARY WIND

And the same day, when the even was come, he saith unto them, Let us pass over unto the other side. And when they had sent away the multitude, they took him even as he was in the ship. And there were also with him other little ships. And there arose a great storm of wind, and the waves beat into the ship, so that it was now full. And he was in the hinder part of the ship, asleep on a pillow: and they awake him, and say unto him, Master, carest thou not that we perish? And he arose, and rebuked the wind, and said unto the sea, Peace, be still. And the wind ceased, and there was a great calm. And he said unto them, Why are ye so fearful? how is it that ye have no faith? And they feared exceedingly, and said one to another, What manner of man is this, that even the wind and the sea obey him? Mark 4:35-41

Contrary wind is an evil wind sent from the camp of the enemy in order to cause sudden problems into the lives and business of the victim. This evil wind blows at a time unexpected. When contrary wind is satanically launched, it goes straight to locate the address of the victim it is programmed against. Contrary wind as the name suggest bring unexpected and unforeseen problems into the business of their victims. The tragedy about this wind is that, it can blow any form of problem into the business and lives of the victim and it will stick until something is quickly done to stop it.

It is good to be spiritually sensitive to know when the enemy is at work to attack your business.

There was a man in the Bible called Job, one day he was in his house when they came to tell him how a contrary wind blew to destroy all the company and success he has built over the years.

And, behold, there came a great wind from the wilderness, and smote the four corners of the house, and it fell upon the young men, and they are dead; and I only am escaped alone to tell thee. Job 1:19

Later the evil wind blew into Job's family and killed all his ten children and his livestock. It closes down the business that Job has taken years to built and brought him completely down in poverty again. Contrary wind, either comes to kill, steal or destroy. Unless such wind are arrested by the power of the Holy Ghost, it will succeed in it operation.

This wind is like when hurricane attacks a city, if it attacks a business, you can imagine what will happen to that business. It will spiritually shut down and physically fizzle out.

Scripture Confession
So shall they fear the name of the LORD from the west, and his glory from the rising of the sun. When the enemy shall come in like a flood, the Spirit of the LORD shall lift up a standard against him. Isa 59:19

They that go down to the sea in ships, that do business in great waters; 24 These see the works of the LORD, and his wonders in the deep. For he commandeth, and raiseth the stormy wind, which lifteth up the waves thereof. They mount up to the heaven, they go down again to the depths:

122

their soul is melted because of trouble. They reel to and fro, and stagger like a drunken man, and are at their wits' end. Then they cry unto the LORD in their trouble, and he bringeth them out of their distresses. He maketh the storm a calm, so that the waves thereof are still. Then are they glad because they be quiet; so he bringeth them unto their desired haven. Oh that [men] would praise the LORD [for] his goodness, and [for] his wonderful works to the children of men! Psalm 107: 23:32

Prayers

1. Oh Lord my father have mercy on me and hear my voice in the name of Jesus.
2. Oh Lord, overturn every contrary wind and it effect in the name of Jesus.
3. Every financial contrary wind blowing against this business cease in the name of Jesus.
4. Every contrary wind blowing against the sales and profit of this business, cease in Jesus name.
5. Every power behind contrary wind blowing against this business, be paralyzed in the name of Jesus.
6. Every source of evil wind, blowing against this business, be destroyed in the name of Jesus.
7. I command an end to contrary winds in Jesus name.
8. Every person of power standing as a contrary wind against this business be disgrace in Jesus name.
9. Every operation of contrary wind against this business be destroyed in the name of Jesus.
10. Let the wind of the Holy Spirit blow restoration and favor back into this business in the name of Jesus.
11. Let the wind of the Lord overshadow this business for a divine turn around in the name of Jesus.

CHAPTER 25

PRAYER AGAINST THE
CLOUD OF DARKNESSS

For, behold, the darkness shall cover the earth, and gross darkness the people: but the LORD shall arise upon thee, and his glory shall be seen upon thee. Isaiah 60:2

Darkness is a strange force and the instrument of the devil to cover good thing from being seen. When darkness covers a business, no awareness and advertisement you will do for the business that will make any impact. It will result to waste of money. Darkness makes something obsolete and desolate.

Darkness is an effort waster. When a business is covered with darkness, every input, skill, ideas, innovation and money that is spent to see the business do well will not yield any positive result, until that darkness is rolled away.

When it was time for God to bring men upon the surface of the earth the first thing He addressed was darkness. The scripture says, and darkness covers the face of the earth, and God commanded light to take over. And John said, light shines in darkness and darkness could not comprehend it.

Darkness always gives way to light. God understand that darkness can covers the glory of something. Darkness hides the beauty, the glamour and the power of a business. Any business under the siege of darkness cannot experience breakthrough. Darkness will silence the testimony of the goods and service of the business. In other word, darkness must not be permitted to stay.

This darkness in quote is not a visible darkness, but a spiritual darkness. When it covers a business, the business will lost it value and becomes a wilderness, a place no one wants to venture into.

Dangers Of Darkness

- Darkness covers the glory of a business from being seen.
- Darkness makes good things to bypass the business.
- Darkness will deny the business of patronage.
- Darkness keeps the business/product/organization out of relevance.
- Darkness steals the identity of the business.
- It makes people forget the business while it is existing.

Scriptural Confession

Arise, shine; for thy light is come, and the glory of the LORD is risen upon thee. For, behold, the darkness shall cover the earth, and gross darkness the people: but the LORD shall arise upon thee, and his glory shall be seen upon thee. And the Gentiles shall come to thy light, and kings to the brightness of thy rising. Isaiah 60:1-3.

In the beginning was the Word, and the Word was with God, and the Word was God. The same was in the beginning with God. All things were made by him; and without him was not anything made that was made. In

him was life; and the life was the light of men. And the light shineth in darkness; and the darkness comprehended it not. John 1:1-5
And have no fellowship with the unfruitful works of darkness, but rather reprove [them]. Eph 5:11

Prayers

1. Every siege of darkness over my life and business, I take authority over you in the name of Jesus and I command you to fade away in Jesus name.
2. Every force of darkness, arresting this business, caging this business, assigned to this business, I decree be evacuated by the force of light in the name of Jesus.
3. Every association of darkness that gathers against this business, scatter in the mighty name of Jesus Christ.
4. Every hand of darkness over this business, over our products and services, I command you to be completely removed in Jesus name.
5. Heaven of deliverance open over this business in the name of Jesus.
6. Angel of deliverance be released over this business in the name of Jesus.
7. Every cloud of darkness covering me and this business I command it to fade away in the name of Jesus.
8. Every covenant of darkness, altar of darkness raised against this business, break off by the power of the Holy Ghost in the name of Jesus Christ.
9. Every agent of darkness, causing disturbances to this business, I command you, be paralyzed in the name of Jesus.

10. Every arrow of darkness that has been released over this business and our products, come out and backfire in Jesus name.

11. Every environmental power assigned to monitor this business be arrested by fire, in the name of Jesus.

12. In the name of Jesus, I separate this business from darkness.

13. In the name of Jesus, I separate my business from the hand of darkness.

14. In the name of Jesus, I separate this business from the operation of darkness.

15. In the name of Jesus, I call my business out of darkness into Christ glorious light.

16. Every stronghold of darkness over and against this business breakthrough, I command the fire of God to locate you and I command you be destroyed by fire in Jesus name.

17. Any coven of darkness where this business has been caged, you that evil coven, hear your judgment vomit this business, and be roasted by the fire of the Holy Ghost.

18. Any weapon of darkness that is in operation against this business, workers, product of this company, stop your operation and be destroyed in the name of Jesus.

19. You my business, company, organization, arise and shine in the name of Jesus.

20. As I have prayed and decree, let it be so in the mighty name of Jesus.

CHAPTER 26

BREAKING OF EVIL PADLOCK

Oh that [men] would praise the LORD [for] his goodness, and [for] his wonderful works to the children of men! For he hath broken the gates of brass, and cut the bars of iron in sunder. Ps 107:15-16.

A padlock is a tool used in locking a door, also used in holding chains that is joined together to tie down an object or wild animal. The physical symbolism of padlock is the spiritual symbolism. Whatever is padlocked can remain like that forever, until a key is brought to unlock the padlock. If the key is misplaced, you will need a strong iron device to break it apart, or an iron cutting device to cut the padlock, each of this format requires rigorous effort.

The same way padlock is used physical, it is also used for wicked spiritual operation, to hold something captives and keep it in bondage forever. As long as the padlock is locked, whatever it is locked against, if it is business that is how it will remained locked until a higher force comes to break it open.

Evil padlock is used to lock up business spiritually from doing well. It is the weapon of the enemy to keep something under compulsory captivity. It takes violent fire-ful and anointed prayer to break this evil padlock operation.

Beloved, it takes only the power of God to break an evil padlock used to lock up a business progress and growth through the force of prayer and fasting.

Signs Of Business Under Padlock Bondage

Such business:

1. Will experience total stagnancy.
2. It will experience round about blockage.
3. It will not enjoy patronage, no matter the quality of the goods, because it has been spiritual padlocked up.
4. It will experience retrogression and setback..
5. It will experience rapid downfall and bankruptcy.
6. It will experience indebtedness upon indebtedness.
7. It will end up in decay of products, and wastage of resources.

Scripture confession: (Personalize it for your business)

And it shall come to pass in the day that the LORD shall give thee rest from thy sorrow, and from thy fear, and from the hard bondage wherein thou waste made to serve, Isa 14:3

No weapon that is formed against thee shall prosper; and every tongue [that] shall rise against thee in judgment thou shalt condemn. This [is] the heritage of the servants of the LORD, and their righteousness [is] of me, saith the LORD. Isa 54:17

Surely [there is] no enchantment against Jacob, neither [is there] any divination against Israel: according to this time it shall be said of Jacob and of Israel, What hath God wrought! Num 23:23

And the Lord shall deliver me from every evil work, and will preserve [me] unto his heavenly kingdom: to whom [be] glory forever and ever. Amen. 2Tim 4:18

Prayers

1. Oh Lord my father, have mercy on me and hear my prayer speedily in Jesus name.

2. Oh Lord my father, release unto me angelic help to break every evil padlock, with the anointing of the Holy Ghost and the power in the name of Jesus.

3. Jesus the yoke breaker, break every evil padlock used to lock the glory of my business in Jesus name.

4. Holy Ghost fire, locate every satanic weapon and device used to tie down my business and destroy them in the name of Jesus.

5. Any evil padlock they have released incantation and enchantment against my business to tie down the business, wherever you are, hear the word of the Lord, In the name of Jesus, break loose and open by fire.

6. Ancestral evil padlock tying down good things in my life and the works of my hand, break in the name of Jesus.

7. Any altar evil padlock is buried against me, wherever you may be, catch fire in the name of Jesus.

8. Oh Lord, my father, unlock every evil padlock used to tie down my business and anything in my life in the name of Jesus.

9. Every operation of evil padlock against my life and business, scatter by fire in the name of Jesus.

10. I lose myself, I lose my business, I lose my products, I lose my money from the bondage of evil padlock in the mighty name of Jesus.

CHAPTER 27

OVERCOMING FRUSTRATION
AND CONFLICTS

Frustration is a product of discouragement after failed attempts; the enemy can trigger you into events that will result into frustration. What frustration does is that it brings confusion and worries. Frustration surface when you are making effort and there is no complimentary outcome. Frustration makes a man to say what he does not mean in the real sense.

After this opened Job his mouth, and cursed his day. And Job spake, and said, Let the day perish wherein I was born, and the night [in which] it was said, There is a man child conceived. Job 3:1-3
Why died I not from the womb? [why] did I [not] give up the ghost when I came out of the belly? Job 3:11

Job spoke heavy words of pains and regret by the reason of frustration. Job 3:1-11. A frustrated man is a bitter man. Frustration is an element of repeated disappointment. If it is not stopped it can lead to depression, then destruction. Through frustration, many people has given up great ideas that should have given them breakthrough. Frustration makes a man to lose confidence in his ability and his idea. When it reaches the peak, it result into breakdown of everything. Your best cannot come out when you are frustrated. Frustration leads to more mistake, error and wrong decision. You can't think straight when you are frustrated. Control yourself when you are frustrated and pray for divine intervention of God to suppress those forces behind your frustration.

Conflicts on it own

Conflicts arise as a result of failed expectation between you and your clients. Conflict if not resolved will escalate to more problem in business. Conflict destroys the potential of any business. Every force behind conflict can be stopped before it succeeds.

Causes Of Frustration

1. Failed promises
2. Failed attempts
3. Failed expectation
4. Failed by trusted people
5. Laboring without profit
6. Disappointment at the edge of breakthrough
7. Slippery breakthrough
8. Repeated failure
9. Manipulation
10. Attacks of darkness
11. Spell
12. Difficulties and hardship
13. Lack and poverty

How to overcome conflict

1. Get relevant knowledge of the causes.
2. Get tips about conflict management.
3. Take your time to resolve it.

4. Pray and fast for the help of the Holy Spirit for few days before taking steps to resolve it.

How To Overcome frustration

1. Have faith in God.
2. Guide your heart.
3. Pray against frustration.
4. Deal with the causes of frustration in your life.

Scriptural confession:

These things I have spoken unto you, that in me ye might have peace. In the world ye shall have tribulation: but be of good cheer; I have overcome the world. John 16:33

Ye are of God, little children, and have overcome them: because greater is he that is in you, than he that is in the world. 1John 4:4

For whatsoever is born of God overcometh the world: and this is the victory that overcometh the world, [even] our faith. 1John 5:4

So shall they fear the name of the LORD from the west, and his glory from the rising of the sun. When the enemy shall come in like a flood, the Spirit of the LORD shall lift up a standard against him. Isa 59:19.

Prayer

1. Every causes of frustration in my life and business, be expose and expire in the name of Jesus.
2. I reject frustration in the name of Jesus.
3. I bind the spirit of frustration in the name of Jesus.
4. Every power point of frustration and conflict, I shut you with the blood of Jesus.

5. Every agent of frustration, I arrest and bind you with the chains of fire in the name of Jesus.
6. Every yoke of frustration be destroyed in Jesus name.
7. Every man or woman behind conflict around this organization let the hand of God touch you and change you for the good of this organization in the name of Jesus.
8. Every wind of conflict cease in the name of Jesus.
9. Every spirit behind conflict, I bind you and cast you out in the name of Jesus.
10. I command an end to every conflict and frustration in my life and this business in the name of Jesus.

CHAPTER 28

PRAYER AGAINST CONSPIRACY

Why do the heathen rage, and the people imagine a vain thing? The kings of the earth set themselves, and the rulers take counsel together, against the LORD, and against his anointed, [saying], Let us break their bands asunder, and cast away their cords from us. Ps 2:1-3

Conspiracy is when fellow business associates gather together against you, just to frustrate your effort and business. You must prepare to overcome it by wisdom and help of God. Conspiracy is bound to happen in business. Conspiracy takes place when you are making it more than them; conspiracy takes place when you don't agree to do business in the worldly way they are doing it, conspiracy is when they are summoning you and challenging you both in the physical realm and spiritual realm. Conspiracy makes some to gain ground and others to enter into their enemies trap and lose their ground. Don't rejoice when people are gathering together against your business.

Effect of conspiracy
1. It can shut down a business, both spiritually and physically.
2. Conspiracy can pull down what one has labored for over the years.
3. Conspiracy can robe you for what you have not done.
4. Conspiracy through it, they can engineer an evil set up.

5. Conspiracy can be used to abort the dream of a business man.
6. It can end a business in court and great loses.

How to handle conspiracy
1. Be strong in the Lord.
2. Know your adversary and their mission.
3. Pray violently and continuously against their plans.

Scriptural confession:
Read whole of Psalm 2.

Associate yourselves, O ye people, and ye shall be broken in pieces; and give ear, all ye of far countries: gird yourselves, and ye shall be broken in pieces; gird yourselves, and ye shall be broken in pieces. Take counsel together, and it shall come to nought; speak the word, and it shall not stand: for God [is] with us. Isa 8:9-10

Behold, they shall surely gather together, [but] not by me: whosoever shall gather together against thee shall fall for thy sake. Isa 54:15.

Who [is] he [that] saith, and it cometh to pass, [when] the Lord commandeth [it] not? Lam 3:37.

Prayers:
1. Oh Lord my father, arise and deliver me from all those who gather against me and my business.
2. Oh Lord, turn all the plans of my conspirators to nothing over me and my business.
3. Every evil set up against my rising up, be aborted in the name of Jesus.

4. Every force behind conspiracy against my business, I dissolve you and your operation in the name of Jesus.

5. Powers of conspirators die in the name of Jesus.

6. Every conspiracy against me die down in the name of Jesus.

7. Every enemy of my business breakthrough be arrested in the name of Jesus.

8. Every satanic network against me, scatter in the name of Jesus.

9. Every satanic agenda and plans against my life and business be aborted in the name of Jesus.

10. Oh Lord, arise and fight for me in the name of Jesus.

11. Pray other prayer as led.

CHAPTER 29

PRAYER AGAINST EVIL ALTARS

But thus shall ye deal with them; ye shall destroy their altars, and break down their images, and cut down their groves, and burn their graven images with fire. Deut 7:5

Altars are a spiritual place of sacrifice, gathering and worship. Every altar has a power base. When an evil altar is contending against a business, it will stagnate and kill the business. Altar is a spiritual force, and also a spiritual point of supernatural operation between the physical and spiritual realm. Evil altar carries power to do havoc against a business.

When an evil altar is contending against any business, the business will be experiencing difficulty, challenges, one problem or the other. The powers on that evil altar will be waging serious war against the success of that business.

Kind Of Altar
1. **Visible altar:** it is the kind you can see with your physical eyes. Like altars in any shrine or satanic gathering.

2. **Invisible altar:** It is an altar your physical eyes cannot see, even though it is real.

Types of altar

1. Divine altar:

Altar of God is the one that the children of God gather to call on God in Holiness. Good example is church altar.

2. Satanic altar

It is an altar where the agent of darkness gathers around to perform evil operation.

Anyone that must wage war against an evil altar successfully must be rooted in Christ. It is only through the power of God in Christ that you can pull down every evil altar and it strongholds.

As ye have therefore received Christ Jesus the Lord, [so] walk ye in him: Rooted and built up in him, and stablished in the faith, as ye have been taught, abounding therein with thanksgiving. Col 2:6-7.

Having God on your side is a victory factor to succeed. No spiritual fight is cheap to win. You can't win a spiritual fight God is not involved in. Understand that God in the midst of his people is mighty, able to save and deliver. And Christ is the head of every principalities and power. With this omnipotent force on your side victory is sure.

How to overcome evil altar

1. Be rooted in Christ.
2. Pray scriptural based prayer.
3. Engage the weapon of fasting.
4. Sow a seed of victory after your prayers

Scriptural confession:

Wherefore God also hath highly exalted him, and given him a name which is above every name: That at the name of Jesus every knee should bow, of [things] in heaven, and [things] in earth, and [things] under the earth; And [that] every tongue should confess that Jesus Christ [is] Lord, to the glory of God the Father. Phil 2:9-11

Prayer

1. Any evil altar that is summoned against my business breakthrough, I pull you down in the name of Jesus.
2. Any voice from evil altar speaking against me, be silenced by the blood of Jesus.
3. Evil altars of my father's house and mothers' house I command you to bow to the name of Jesus.
4. Any one that has consulted any evil altar against me and my business be exposed and disgraced in the name of Jesus.
5. Every foundational and ancestral evil altar causing negative influence against me be destroyed in Jesus name
6. Any evil sacrifice made on evil altar against my business, catch fire in the name of Jesus.
7. Any token that has been given on any evil altar against my business, be destroyed in the name of Jesus.
8. I command all the operation of evil altar against my business to cease in the name of Jesus.
9. Every attack from evil altars against my business, backfire in the name of Jesus.
10. I pulled down the horns of darkness raised against my business in the name of Jesus.
11. I cover my business with the blood of Jesus.

CHAPTER 30

BREAKING OF HIDDEN CURSES

Now in the morning as he returned into the city, he hungered. And when he saw a fig tree in the way, he came to it, and found nothing thereon, but leaves only, and said unto it, Let no fruit grow on thee henceforward forever. And presently the fig tree withered away. And when the disciples saw [it], they marvelled, saying, How soon is the fig tree withered away! Matthew. 21: 18-20.

Curse looks so casual and yet can destroy the seed of a business. If a business is cursed, it cannot survive. Curse is a negative words carrying evil power issued with the purpose of destroying, condemning, killing and perverting the fruitfulness of a business. Whatever curse is upon will go contrary to how it is doing. If it is growing, it will start dying. If it's making money, it will start accumulating debt and loses. If people are coming to patronize the business, it will just become desolate. That is when a curse at work. You don't joke with the efficacy of a curse, you break it.

Effect of curse on business
- Curse can bring wrong workers.
- Curse can keep business in bondage.
- Curse will create a loophole that will be making the business owners to be spending without making profit.

141

- Curse will make business to run at lost.
- Curse will make a business to close down.
- Curse can also make the business to be experiencing rising and falling.
- Curse can make a strange happening to be occurring regularly or seasonally.

Type of curses
1. Generational curse
2. Ancestral evil curse
3. Parental curse
4. Self imposed curse
5. Satanic curse

How curses are incurred
1. Breaking of covenants. Jer. 11:3
2. Disobedience to God. 1Sam. 15:22-28
3. Embezzling tithes and offering. Mal. 3:8-9
4. Inheritance: e.g like the case of Gehazi. 2kings 5:27.
5. Self imposed curses. Jer. 2:17
6. Rape, extra-marital sex, premarital sex. Deut. 27:20-23
7. Stealing, robbery, fraud, injustice etc. Prov. 3:33
8. Dishonoring your parents. Deut. 27:16
9. Rewarding evil for good. Prov. 17:13
10. Practicing incest. Deut. 27:20,22
11. Lying with a beast (animals) Deut. 27:21
12. Blaspheming the name of God. Lev. 24:15-16
13. Deception. Joshua 9:22-23
14. Offending those in authority…like a priest, a king, a pastor etc.

How to nullify curse

1. Confess every sin that could bring any curse and judgment.
2. If possible make restitution or amendment where necessary.
3. Engage the blood of Jesus to cleanse yourself.
4. Pray using the word to nullify every curse and it effect in your life and business.

Scriptural declaration

Christ hath redeemed us from the curse of the law, being made a curse for us: for it is written, Cursed [is] every one that hangeth on a tree:
That the blessing of Abraham might come on the Gentiles through Jesus Christ; that we might receive the promise of the Spirit through faith. Gal 3:13-14

As the bird by wandering, as the swallow by flying, so the curse causeless shall not come. Prov. 26:2

I will overturn, overturn, overturn, it: and it shall be no [more], until he come whose right it is; and I will give it [him]. Ezek 21:27.

Prayer

1. Oh Lord, forgive me of any sin, error and mistake that has brought curse upon this business in Jesus name.
2. Oh Lord, let your mercy overrule every judgment of curses in my life in Jesus name.
3. Any curse that is affecting my business breakthrough be cancelled by the blood of Jesus.
4. Every inherited curse causing damage to my success be destroyed by the blood of Jesus.

5. Every evil altar backing curse in my life and business be roasted by the fire of the Holy Ghost in Jesus name.

6. Any evil voice raining curse upon my business, I command the curse to back fire in the name of Jesus.

7. I break every hold of curses over my business in Jesus name.

8. Every self imposed curse in my life, be cancelled by the blood of Jesus.

9. I turn every curse in my life and business to blessing in the name of Jesus.

10. I command the effect of every curse to expire in the name of Jesus.

11. I declare myself curse free, and I declare my business curse free in the name of Jesus.

12. I command the blessing of God from above to overshadow my life and business in Jesus name.

13. Every demon of curse attach to my life, I disconnect you with the blood of Jesus.

14. I command the blessing of God upon my life and business in the name of Jesus.

REMOVING BARRIERS,
OBSTACLES AND LIMITATION

Wherefore we would have come unto you, even I Paul, once and again; but Satan hindered us. 1Thess 2:18

Barriers are this seen forces that are standing as a physical obstruction to the progress of something. Barrier can be human agent, spiritual or physical roadblock, negative rules and regulation that is affecting the business progress.

Obstacles are the spiritual hindrances, spiritual evil manipulation to hinder good things from materializing.

When there is a barrier and obstacles, then it will lead to limitation. Limitation means to peg the progress of something to a spot. Despite making all possible effort, the business, sales is still limited to certain number. It has never passed that number over the years. Limitation is the enemy of advancement. And when the operation of limitation is at work for too much a long time, it will lead to permanent stagnation.

Scripture confession
Wherefore God also hath highly exalted him, and given him a name which is above every name: That at the name of Jesus every knee should bow, of

[things] in heaven, and [things] in earth, and [things] under the earth;
And [that] every tongue should confess that Jesus Christ [is] Lord, to the
glory of God the Father. Phil 2:9-11

Then he answered and spake unto me, saying, This [is] the word of the
LORD unto Zerubbabel, saying, Not by might, nor by power, but by my
spirit, saith the LORD of hosts. Who [art] thou, O great mountain?
before Zerubbabel [thou shalt become] a plain: and he shall bring forth the
headstone [thereof with] shoutings, [crying], Grace, grace unto it. Zech 4:6-7

Casting down imaginations, and every high thing that exalteth itself against
the knowledge of God, and bringing into captivity every thought to the
obedience of Christ; 2Cor 10:5

Prayers

1. Oh Lord, release your spirit to help us remove every obstacles, obstruction, roadblocks, hindrances, limitations causing failure in the name of Jesus.
2. Every object of limitation opposing the growth of this business, be removed and destroyed in the name of Jesus.
3. Every known and unknown obstacles standing against this business, be removed by the force of the Holy Ghost in Jesus name.
4. Anointing to destroy every yoke of limitation I command it upon this business in the name of Jesus.
5. I remove obstacles, hindrances and limitation in the name of Jesus.
6. Let the way be clear completely for this business in the name of Jesus.

CHAPTER 32

PRAYER FOR DIVINE ENLARGEMENT

Enlarge the place of thy tent, and let them stretch forth the curtains of thine habitations: spare not, lengthen thy cords, and strengthen thy stakes; For thou shalt break forth on the right hand and on the left; and thy seed shall inherit the Gentiles, and make the desolate cities to be inhabited. Is. 54:2-3

Every business must grow to a point where it will require it enlargement. No business is meant to stay the same. Thou your beginning may be small but your end shall be great. That is enlargement confession. It started small yesterday, is growing now, and has need that the board, owners must come together and plan for it enlargement.

Enlargement is a product of planning and favor. Every growing venture, expanding and enlarging has a force making it to work within or without. However prayer is a spiritual force that is available to help you to enlarge your business. You may not have access to every other force, but you have access to the force of prayer. Prayer works to your advantage. Every business man must build a prayer altar.

The scripture above says, enlarge the place of your tent (business) and let them stretch forth the curtains of thine habitation (location).

The word is a given command, inspired by the Spirit of the Lord, the scripture further says, all things are possible to him that believes. Every word of God carries a possibility power to those who key into the written word. The word is not weak, it is active, full of life and Spirit. You must make a move to enlarge your business input, and space. The word of God says as you do so, you shall break forth on the right side and on the left side. God has spoken, blessed are those who believe. Move on that word to expand the business, you can open another branch of your business in another location.

Why The Business Need Divine Enlargement

1. It makes the business go global.
2. It makes the business a blessing to his community by employing more people in a generation where many people are looking for jobs to survive.
3. It increases the gross income of the business.
4. It gives the business power to become more.
5. It put the business in a position to boost the economy of his country.
6. To bring fulfillment and accomplishment.

Scriptural confession:

Ah Lord GOD! behold, thou hast made the heaven and the earth by thy great power and stretched out arm, [and] there is nothing too hard for thee: Jer 32:17

And Jesus looking upon them saith, With men [it is] impossible, but not with God: for with God all things are possible. Mark 10:27

Now unto him that is able to do exceeding abundantly above all that we ask or think, according to the power that worketh in us, Eph 3:20

Prayers:

1. Oh Lord God, the earth is yours and the fullness thereof, release upon this business the grace for enlargement in Jesus name.

2. Obstacles to our business enlargement be revealed and removed in the name of Jesus.

3. The power of God for divine enlargement fall upon this business in the name of Jesus.

4. The perfect innovation for enlargement be revealed to me in Jesus name.

5. Doors of divine enlargement open unto this business in the name of Jesus.

6. Anointing of God for divine enlargement fall on this business in the name of Jesus.

7. The grace for unlimited enlargement, expansion and multiplication fall on this business in the name of Jesus.

8. Any human agent or demonic agent that want to manipulate, stop or delay this enlargement plans, be uprooted out of your place in the name of Jesus.

9. I command the enlargement of this business in the name of the Lord Jesus Christ. Amen

10. Thank you Jesus for answered prayers.

STAGE 4
Personal Prayer For The Business Man

CHAPTER 33

PRAYER FOR DIVINE DIRECTION

I will instruct thee and teach thee in the way which thou shalt go: I will guide thee with mine eye. Ps 32:8
And thine ears shall hear a word behind thee, saying, This [is] the way, walk ye in it, when ye turn to the right hand, and when ye turn to the left. Isa 30:21

Divine direction is God telling you what to do, where to do it, and how to do it. Divine direction is the full backing of God to ensure you become an eternal success in the business.

Every business man needs personal instruction from above to guide him start the business from the scratch and take it to the top. You can't run a successful business with common sense. God knows the steps and direction you must take to get to your wealthy place. The easiest way to get it right in business is to be led by the Spirit of God. God cannot make a mistake. Divine direction practically get God involve in all your business activities. It reveals where the business should be located, who you should partner with, when to invest and when not to invest.

Divine direction will give you clear picture of where to sources for your raw materials, who to supply and who to deal with to make profit. He knows the end from the beginning. Divine direction will keep you in the light of God's guidance and

151

instruction. And it will save you from wrong investment, loses and wrong steps in business.

VEHICLES OF DIVINE DIRECTION

1. Dream: Job 33:14-18.
2. Vision: Act 10:3, Act 2:17
3. Voice of the spirit: Isaiah 30:21
4. Through prophets: 2kings 5:9-15.

Scriptural confession:
Trust in the LORD with all thine heart; and lean not unto thine own understanding. In all thy ways acknowledge him, and he shall direct thy paths. Prov 3:5-6
Call unto me, and I will answer thee, and shew thee great and mighty things, which thou knowest not. Jer. 33:3

Prayer
1. Holy Spirit, I invite you, I submit myself to your leadership, take over now in the name of Jesus.
2. Oh Lord, direct my step on what and what to do at this time on this business
3. Open my eyes to see and my hears to receive the instruction awaiting me in the name of Jesus.
4. I command destruction against all spiritual obstruction to my reception in the name of Jesus.
5. I activate my spirit man to come alive to receive from God in the name of Jesus.

CHAPTER 34

PRAYER FOR BAPTISM OF GIFTS

Thou hast ascended on high, thou hast led captivity captive: **thou hast received gifts for men***; yea, [for] the rebellious also, that the* LORD *God might dwell [among them].* Ps 68:18

The kingdom of God operates with different gifts. Gift is given to believers to become the light of the world. It is the gift of God in you that brings your manifestation out as the sons of God. You cannot make a difference without having relevant gift of God operating in you.

A man's gift maketh room for him, and bringeth him before great men.
Prov 18:16

There are diverse spiritual gift. Spiritual gift makes one's work to be significant. These gifts are given by God to be a special added value to your business endeavour.

You must be an active carrier of the gift of the spirit to be in command of situations. Receiving of divine direction is easy when you are possessed with relevant spiritual gift. A believer without spiritual gift is still in the dark. It is the possession of those gift that will connect your spiritual antenna to the media house of heaven to receive expressly what is about to happen, what you need to know.

Your gift is your channel of good news, information, direction, and revelation. The gift of the spirit is given by the Holy Spirit.

Benefits Of Spiritual Gift

1. It makes you know things before they happen. Act.2:17
2. It gives you power to change situation. Luke 10:19
3. It makes you a priest in the market place. Rev. 1:6
4. It makes you a light of your world. Matthew 5:13-16
5. It makes you produce excellent result. Dan. 5:12
6. It makes you fruitful. John 15:16
7. It makes you a compass to others. Isaiah 30:21

Some of the gift

1. *Gift of Vision. Joel 2:28*
2. *Gift of Dreams. Act. 2:17*
3. *Gift of the spirit of Prophecy. Act 2:17*
4. *Gift of Power. Luke 10:19*
5. *Gift of hearing. Isaiah 30:21*
6. *Gift of Skill. Dan. 9:22*
7. *Gift of knowledge, wisdom and understanding. Isaiah 11:2*
8. *Gift of discernment. Ezek. 44:23*
9. *Outpouring of the anointing. Ps. 23:5*

Scriptural confession:

And it shall come to pass in the last days, saith God, I will pour out of my Spirit upon all flesh: and your sons and your daughters shall prophesy, and

your young men shall see visions, and your old men shall dream dreams:
Acts 2:17

Prayers

1. Oh Lord, sanctify me with your blood in Jesus name.
2. Doors of spiritual gift, be open unto me in the name of Jesus.
3. Anything in my body and environment making me to be spiritually unreachable for possessing the gifts, be removed and roasted by fire in the name of Jesus.
4. Blood of Jesus clean my spiritual pipe in the name of Jesus.
5. Oh Lord, give me new spiritual receiver in Jesus name.
6. Oh Lord, release upon me the grace needed to possess all the gift relevant for me in business in Jesus name.
7. Power of the Holy Ghost, my life is available possess me in Jesus name.
8. Lord Jesus, fill me with the gift of visions, dreams, prophecy, discernment etc in the name of Jesus.
9. I activate all this gift in my life henceforth in the name of Jesus.
10. Oh Lord my father, fill me with the spirit of wisdom, knowledge and understanding in Jesus name.

PRAYER FOR MERCY AND FAVOR
OF GOD

For I desired mercy, and not sacrifice; and the knowledge of God more than burnt offerings. Hos. 6:6.

The mercy and the favor of God goes together. It takes mercy to receive from God. When God wants to favor a man, he employs the vehicle of mercy, so that all his accuser will be silenced. Since mercy rejoice over judgment, and God is the custodian of mercy, when a man finds God's mercy he will walk in liberty, and his adversaries will not be able to do anything.

LORD, by thy favour thou hast made my mountain to stand strong: thou didst hide thy face, [and] I was troubled. Ps 30:7

You cannot go far without the mercy of God. It is God mercy that makes you rejoice over the works of your hands.

For he saith to Moses, I will have mercy on whom I will have mercy, and I will have compassion on whom I will have compassion. So then [it is] not of him that willeth, nor of him that runneth, but of God that sheweth mercy. Rom 9:15-16.

Without God's mercy your struggle will multiply, you will struggle to achieve every single thing, and you will think that is the way you are created to struggle. But when mercy and favors shows up, it takes away the struggle and makes it easy to get all you are struggling to achieve easily.

When you see a man doing well in business and enjoying it, it is because mercy and favor of God is not lacking in his live. Don't envy anyone enjoying mercy and favor of God, tap into your own grace of mercy and favor through prayer and fasting.

When the Lord has concluded to favor you, He will show you mercy to qualify you for the favor. God show his mercy to those who desire it passionate.

The LORD taketh pleasure in them that fear him, in those that hope in his mercy. Ps 147:11.

Every business person needs the mercy and favor of God. When mercy and favor has finished your work, your life will become enviable. However, know that God always desire to show mercy and favor on his children who believes and hope for his mercy.

Effect of mercy
1. Mercy will overrule all your past mistakes, sins and blunders.
2. Mercy will make you a candidate for God's favor.
3. Mercy makes you walk in freedom.
4. Mercy paralyses the decisions of your enemy.

5. Mercy makes God your voice.
6. Mercy makes you acceptable before God and man.
7. Mercy make God cut off your enemies and their works in your life. Ps. 143:12

Effect of favor

1. Favor makes you the best choice.
2. Favor makes you a celebrity.
3. Favor attracts good things to your life.
4. Favor increases your substances, resources, provision.
5. Favor opens doors for you.
6. Favor pronounces your work.
7. Favor makes you the choice to be blessed by men and God.
8. Favor makes you find mercy and help.
9. Favor has a way of making things work.
10. Favor makes goodness radiate around you.
11. Favor makes you the candidate for testimony.
12. Favor makes you stand out.

Scriptural confession

But as for me, I will come [into] thy house in the multitude of thy mercy: [and] in thy fear will I worship toward thy holy temple. Ps 5:7

Remember not the sins of my youth, nor my transgressions: according to thy mercy remember thou me for thy goodness' sake, O LORD. Ps 25:7

Hear, O LORD, and have mercy upon me: LORD, be thou my helper. Ps 30:10

Let thy mercy, O LORD, be upon us, according as we hope in thee. Ps 33:22

O turn unto me, and have mercy upon me; give thy strength unto thy servant, and save the son of thine handmaid. Ps 86:16

And of thy mercy cut off mine enemies, and destroy all them that afflict my soul: for I [am] thy servant. Ps 143:12

Prayer
1. Oh Lord, show me mercy in the name of Jesus.
2. Oh Lord, overshadow my life with the canopy of your mercy in the name of Jesus.
3. Oh Lord, release the oil of mercy on me in the name of Jesus.
4. Anointing of favor fall upon me in the name of Jesus.
5. Doors of mercy and favor open unto me in the name of Jesus.
6. Favor of God for global breakthrough fall upon my life in the name of Jesus.
7. Every anti favor spirit, marks, power in operation against my life, be uprooted by fire in the name of Jesus.
8. Wind of favor blow into my life in the name of Jesus.
9. Thank you Jesus for answered prayer.

CHAPTER 36

DELIVERANCE PRAYERS
FROM AFFLICTION

Many [are] the afflictions of the righteous: but the LORD delivereth him out of them all. Ps 34:19

Afflictions are evil projections launched into the life of a person. Affliction is a satanic attack that is unleashed against a person to keep them in captivity and their health in bondage. Any business person can be a victim of satanic affliction, it does not cause for fear and timidity, it only calls for you to stand on your ground and call on God. One of the ways the enemy gains upper hand over their adversary is to afflict them with sickness, disease, infirmity, one major problem or the other to shift their focus away from their enterprise, and begin to nurse the affliction.

The word of God has revealed to us that many are the afflictions of the righteous but the Lord delivers him out of them all. If yours is only one affliction, the Lord will easily deliver you.

Don't undermine any affliction, whatever is the affliction the enemy has launched against you to keep you in perpetual pain, and fear, making you to waste your resources, the Lord has assured deliverance. Every affliction is the product of the devil, if the devil succeeds in afflicting you and you keep silent, you will give him an upper hand. You must send back every affliction to the pit of hell where it came from.

The word of God says.

For he hath not despised nor abhorred the affliction of the afflicted; neither hath he hid his face from him; but when he cried unto him, he heard. Ps 22:24

God does not despise you in your affliction, His face is not hidden, He is only waiting for your prayer. Whatever you reject God will reject it with you. You must stand on God's word to put an end to every affliction in your life. However prayer is the cure for affliction.

Is any among you afflicted? let him pray. *Is any merry? let him sing psalms. Jas 5:13*

If you can declare a prayer of faith over the affliction in the next 7 days, the affliction will dry up instantly by the power of God.

Signs of affliction
1. Terrible sickness or disease e.g cancer, stroke etc.
2. Constant attack on your health.
3. Having strange feelings or movement in your body.

Scriptural Confession
And the Lord shall deliver me from every evil work, and will preserve [me] unto his heavenly kingdom: to whom [be] glory forever and ever. Amen. 2Tim 4:18

Is any among you afflicted? Let him pray. Is any merry? Let him sing psalms. Jas 5:13.

Heal me, O LORD, and I shall be healed; save me, and I shall be saved: for thou [art] my praise. Jer 17:14, Read also Psalm 102:1-28.

Prayers

1. Oh Lord, power belongs to you, arise in your power and put an end to all the affliction in my life.
2. Oh Lord, touch me and heal me in the name of Jesus.
3. Anointing of healing fall upon me in the name of Jesus.
4. Every arrows of affliction in my life come out and backfire in the name of Jesus.
5. Every plantation in my body causing affliction, it is written that what my heavenly father has not planted in me shall be uprooted, I command you to be uprooted from the root in the name of Jesus.
6. Altar of affliction raised against me, be destroyed by the fire of the Holy Ghost in the name of Jesus.
7. Any power, familiar spirit, satanic agent satanically assigned to afflict me, I bind you and terminate your operation in my life in the name of Jesus.
8. Every seed of affliction in my life, wither in the name of Jesus.
9. Every pollution in my system sustaining this affliction, drain out by the authority in the name of Jesus.
10. Blood of Jesus flush out every affliction in my body and my life in the name of Jesus.
11. Every long time affliction of sickness, disease, cancer and infirmity, I flush you out with the blood of Jesus.

12. Every cause of affliction in my life be exposed and destroyed by the authority in the name of Jesus.

13. Every stubborn yoke of affliction, be destroyed in the name of Jesus.

14. Every Satanic gadget monitoring me in order to afflict me, I send the fire of God upon you, be consumed by the fire of the Holy Ghost in the name of Jesus.

15. It is written; from hence forth let no one trouble me for I bear in my body the mark of the Lord Jesus Christ. Mark of the Lord for protection from attacks come upon me in the name of Jesus.

16. Oh Lord, command deliverance for me in the name of Jesus.

17. Thank you Lord, for answered prayers in the name of Jesus.

CHAPTER 37

PRAYER AGAINST DEATH ATTACK

Thou shalt come to [thy] grave in a full age, like as a shock of corn cometh in his season.
Lo this, we have searched it, so it [is]; hear it, and know thou [it] for thy good. Job 5:26-27

Death is imminent; however God does not design early death for any man without accomplishing his mission on earth. God is against all that is against you. And God has put in place checks and measures against every satanic attacks, affliction and evil agenda against his children.

Sudden death is a tragedy, not a testimony. God does not want the sudden death of anyone, and so God will readily intervene and deliver his children from the claws of untimely death. God has given you life that supersedes death through Christ so that death will not have power over you. By knowledge shall the just be delivered.

And I give unto them eternal life; and they shall never perish, neither shall any [man] pluck them out of my hand. My Father, which gave [them] me, is greater than all; and no [man] is able to pluck [them] out of my Father's hand. I and [my] Father are one. John 10:28-30

God has passed unto you life through Christ by the virtue of this life, you are not permitted to die untimely, death does not have power over your life. *Jesus said, you will never perish, neither shall any man pluck you out of my hands.*

Mark this word of Christ carefully, you will never perish, he is not making a boast but he was simply giving you insight into the kind of life he brought for you. It is a life that cannot be killed. You will never perish simply means your soul will not end in hell, but in the kingdom of heaven. Eternal life is not a life that can be terminated by terminal diseases, affliction, attacks, evil arrow, oppression or any of its kind. Arise and shake out every arrow of death in you in Jesus name.

And he also said, *neither shall any (man) pluck you out of my hand*, man is in bracket, but any is the key word. Any will not pluck you out of my hands. Any there means, whether man, whether the devil, whether sickness, none of those things that take men's life before their time will ever have power over you, because you have a greater life in you, a life that cannot be killed.

No one can pluck you out of the hand of Christ, because God is the shield and buckler of every man in Christ and no one can be snatched out of the hands of God. Who is it that says a thing and it comes to pass when the Lord has not commanded? Lam. 3:37. It is only God that has the final say. He has the power to kill and to bring back to life. *but the people that do know their God shall be strong, and do [exploits]. Dan 11:32*

The life in Christ is a divine insurance for the righteous.

How to be delivered from the claw of death?

1. **Surrender your life to Jesus:** John 3:16
    When you surrender your life, he will take it and give you new life that is higher than death.

2. **Get a bible to seek the knowledge of God: Acts.17:11**
    Get yourself a new bible; mark out scriptures that speak about victory over death. Knowledge is the first weapon of deliverance, before faith and prayer finalize the work.

3. **Leave a consecrated life: 1Pet. 1:15-16**
    Sin is a platform through which doors are open to the devil to have a legal right to operate and oppress the people of God

4. **Pray violent against every verdict of death: Job 22:28**
    You shall decree a thing and it shall be established by God.

Scriptures confession
Since thou wast precious in my sight, thou hast been honourable, and I have loved thee: therefore will I give men for thee, and people for thy life. Isa 43:4
For thou hast delivered my soul from death, mine eyes from tears, [and] my feet from falling.
I will walk before the LORD in the land of the living. Ps 116:8-9
The voice of rejoicing and salvation [is] in the tabernacles of the righteous: the right hand of the LORD doeth valiantly. The right hand of the LORD is exalted: the right hand of the LORD doeth valiantly. I shall not die, but live, and declare the works of the LORD. Ps 118:15-17

The name of the LORD [is] a strong tower: the righteous runneth into it, and is safe. Prov. 18:10

Prayers:
1. Oh Lord hear my voice in the day of trouble, by your mercy answer me speedily in the name of Jesus.
2. Every covenant of death, operating against my life and existence, I disannul you in the name of Jesus.
3. Every where they gather against me to see my end, let the Lord arise as a consuming fire and scatter them in the name of Jesus.
4. Oh Lord, deliver me and be my refuge from every plans and arrangement of untimely death in the name of Jesus.
5. Every hanging judgment of death over my life be cancelled by the power in the blood of Jesus.
6. Oh Lord, redeem my life with your blood from every concluded works of death in the name of Jesus.
7. I decree, that every power of death over my life, loose hold on me in the mighty name of Jesus Christ.
8. I command every fear of death to disappear in the name of Jesus.
9. I cancel every dream of death by the blood of Jesus.
10. I declare any event that has been program one way or the other to cause untimely death in my life, be aborted in the name of Jesus.
11. Arrows of untimely death fired into my life, back fire in the name of Jesus.
12. Every seed of death program into my body die in the name of Jesus.
13. Every sickness of death in my body, I am not a candidate of untimely death, come out and die in Jesus name.

14. Oh Lord, deliver me from every form of sudden death in the name of Jesus.
15. Any one monitoring me to kill me, oh Lord, let them die in my place in the name of Jesus.
16. I will not walk into where death is waiting in the name of Jesus.
17. Oh Lord, release your angel to keep guide over me in the name of Jesus.
18. I will not go on a journey of no return in the name of Jesus.
19. I am covered with the blood of Jesus.
20. Angel of life from the Lord, preserve me in the name of Jesus.

CHAPTER 38

PRAYER FOR NEW IDEAS, INNOVATION AND DIVINE CONNECTION

John answered and said, A man can receive nothing, except it be given him from heaven. John 3:27

Idea is a gift from God to bless the life of men. Idea is released by the inspiration of the Spirit of God. It takes a powerful idea to take your world by storm. Every idea has a voice. Idea is different from career. Idea is a divine gift that comes from heaven into the mind of whom God has delighted to execute such idea through. One of the major way idea is conceived is through demand. If there is no demand for it, there may be no supply from heaven.

Every good gift and every perfect gift is from above, and cometh down from the Father of lights, with whom is no variableness, neither shadow of turning. Jas 1:17

Few people make demand for divine idea. Every good gift and perfect gift comes from above. Every idea from above is divine and it is a blessing. Whatever idea God have released into your hands will usher you into lasting success and prosperity. One powerful idea has the power to change your life for good and forever. Divine idea will bring you before nobles.

169

A man's gift maketh room for him, and bringeth him before great men. Prov 18:16.

A gift [is as] a precious stone in the eyes of him that hath it: whithersoever it turneth, it prospereth. Prov 17:8

God give idea to people to prosper them on earth. God is full of ideas, you have a free access to approach him and make your demand. When a man's time has come, God will stir up in him divine idea to bless him.

God is responsible for everyone he created and it is God's responsibility to supply to men the idea he needs to pursue the dreams of his life. It is mandatory to seek the face of God for a generational business idea.

When God open a man's eyes and his mind, he will see many life changing ideas and opportunity around him.

Innovation:
Innovation is adding unique values to give your idea an edge among it contemporaries. It is a deep insight. The idea is the seed. You need eyes for innovation to see new innovative side of an idea. Innovation is a product of wisdom and knowledge, which all comes from God. Don't forget, God owns everything, when men is no more on earth, all things still remain his, however he has no need for them. Idea is one of the vehicles of divine sustenance. A great idea open doors to people and connect them to people and places they would not have known all their life.

Divine connection:

It is when God connect you to those who matter to see you through in life. god can connect you to those who will help you achieve your dreams and achieve. God can also connect you to those who will give you the platform to be useful in life. Divine connection launches you to another dimension of opportunity to succeed without sweat and struggle.

How to generate idea?
1. Invite the Holy Spirit through worship.
2. Ask for it in prayer passionately.
3. Wait on the Lord in meditation.

Benefit of divine connection
1. It helps you to find relevant support to carry out your ideas.
2. It opens doors of help and helpers to you.
3. It makes you connect to people that can help you to give birth to that idea in a unique way.

Scriptural confession:
1. Oh Lord, open the doors of idea to me in Jesus name.
2. Those ideas you have prepared for me release it to me in Jesus name.
3. Whatever can stand has an obstruction to my receiving of what you have for me, oh Lord, take it out of the way.
4. I ask for grace for uncommon innovation to maximize the idea to greater level in Jesus name.
5. Oh Lord, open the doors of divine connection to me in the name of Jesus.

6. Oh Lord my father, through this ideas, connect me to places and people relevant to my goals in life in the name of Jesus.

7. Oh Lord, give me the wisdom to utilize this idea to the maximal level in the name of Jesus.

8. Every provision needed to establish this idea, provide them all in the name of Jesus.

9. Anointing for new ideas, innovation and divine connection, fall upon me and begin to manifest in the name of Jesus.

CHAPTER 39

PRAYER FOR THE POWER TO MAKE WEALTH

But thou shalt remember the LORD thy God: for [it is] he that giveth thee power to get wealth, that he may establish his covenant which he sware unto thy fathers, as [it is] this day. Deut 8:18

Wealth flow is a mystery and this is the mystery of wealth making. Wealth is the highest level of financial and material acquisition. Wealth is given by God, and the measure through which God release the wealth into your life is by giving you a powerful idea and opportunity, and then crowning it with the power to make wealth. Idea is not enough, opportunity can bring you some goodies, but not wealth as such, but when this great anointing comes upon you with just a little idea, the wealth that follows will be unimaginable. However, wealth acquired through dubious medium is a curse. God is against accurse wealth.

[As] the partridge sitteth [on eggs], and hatcheth [them] not; [so] he that getteth riches, and not by right, shall leave them in the midst of his days, and at his end shall be a fool. Jer 17:11

God is not in support of illegal way of acquiring riches and fortune. There is judgments that await the acquiring of wealth in any ungodly means. Wherefore, God is ready to give you wealth in the right way.

It is God that gives a man the power to get wealth. If the power is not there, Strategy cannot create wealth, it takes that power only which God is willing to freely give. Power for wealth is needed for wealth to find it way into your life. This power is a spiritual magnetic force that draws wealth and riches into your life. It obeys the command of God on your life. When God is ready to change your status he releases upon you power to make wealth. God delights in solving every problem of financial hardship in your life.

And I will give thee the treasures of darkness, and hidden riches of secret places, that thou mayest know that I, the LORD, which call [thee] by thy name, [am] the God of Israel. Isa 45:3.

God delight in blessing his own, so he has made the power available through Christ, that the blessing of Abraham may be made manifest in the life of everyone who believes in Jesus. Gal. 3:13-14

He says, he will give you the treasures of darkness, and hidden riches of secret places. No one knows where riches is hidden, but when the Lord is at work in your life, through his anointing, he command the hidden riches to find its way to you.

It does not matter the place you live, the remote area you are operating your business, riches is hidden everywhere, it only takes God to command it to locate you.

Requirement For Receiving
1. Give Your Life To Jesus.
2. Have A Genuine Desire For It.
3. Ask For It In Faith.

Scriptural confession:
And the sons of strangers shall build up thy walls, and their kings shall minister unto thee: for in my wrath I smote thee, but in my favour have I had mercy on thee.

Therefore thy gates shall be open continually; they shall not be shut day nor night; that [men] may bring unto thee the forces of the Gentiles, and [that] their kings [may be] brought. Isa 60:10-11

Thou shalt also suck the milk of the Gentiles, and shalt suck the breast of kings: and thou shalt know that I the LORD [am] thy Saviour and thy Redeemer, the mighty One of Jacob.

For brass I will bring gold, and for iron I will bring silver, and for wood brass, and for stones iron: I will also make thy officers peace, and thine exactors righteousness. Isa 60:16-17.

1. Oh Lord, release upon me the power to make wealth in the name of Jesus.
2. Oh Lord, release upon my business the power to attract wealth making profit in the name of Jesus.
3. Oh Lord, open unto me the door and channels of wealth in the name of Jesus.
4. Any anti prosperity curse in my life, be nullified in the name of Jesus.
5. Oh Lord, command unending flow of wealth into my life and business in the name of Jesus.

CHAPTER 40

BREAKING THE YOKE
OF BUSINESS FAILURE

For it shall come to pass in that day, saith the LORD of hosts, [that] I will break his yoke from off thy neck, and will burst thy bonds, and strangers shall no more serve themselves of him: Jer 30:8

If your business and destiny is tied to failure, it is time to separate it from failure by removing the yoke. Failure means to be making effort without getting the desired result. Failure comes in different shape and sizes. Failure leads to frustration, and repeated failure leads to loss of hope. Failure is meant to challenge you and make you stronger, and eventually lead you to success. But if failure remains resolute and ultimate in your business and effort, it means you need to give it a prayer attention.

If God did not intervene in some people's failure experience, they will never have a thirst of success. One of the avenue of escaping the trap of failure is divine intervention by prayer.

Kinds of failure

1. **Normal failure:**

   Normal failure is a natural failure. Virtually everyone experience it at one time or the other. When you are experiencing natural failure, after making attempt a few times, it will give way to success. Normal failure occurs as a result of just trying something the first time, without mastering the art yet. It can also be as a result of mistake and error. But after all what is needed has been put in place and mastered, then success will show up easily.

2. Abnormal failure:

Abnormal failure is when all methods has failed, all strategies and plans has refused to yield result, all training and skill acquired in order to succeed amount to nothing. It is chronic in nature and it can be provocative. It seems the more you try the more the failure is showing up.

Others tried once, twice and thrice and made it. But you have tried several times without a thirst of success, you have changed strategy and you are still meeting failure, it is abnormal, it needs immediate prayer attention. Abnormal failure can also be termed demonic failure. Whatever is abnormal is demonic. It needs divine intervention to turn it around.

3. Hereditary failure:

This is a failure from generation to generation. It is a pattern of failure in the family where no one succeeds. The junction the grandfather failed is the junction the father failed, the junction the father failed is the same junction the son is failing. Like father like son kind of failure. The evil hereditary failure pattern must break in Jesus name.

You have a choice to put a end to every failure in your life.

Sign of business failure

1. Sudden collapse of business.
2. Rising and falling in the business.
3. Stagnation.
4. Disappointment.
5. Wrong partnership.
6. Wrong investment.
7. Failed effort and attempt.
8. Repeated disappointment.
9. Inability to make headway after much effort.

How To Break The Yoke Of Business Failure

1. Find out the possible causes of failure.
2. Write out how to overcome.
3. Embark on prayers and fasting to deal with every active cause of failure. Is. 58:6.
4. Do all over again till something positive happens.

Scriptural confession:

For whatsoever is born of God overcometh the world: and this is the victory that overcometh the world, [even] our faith. Who is he that overcometh the world, but he that believeth that Jesus is the Son of God? 1John 5:4-5
And he said, The things which are impossible with men are possible with God. Luke 18:27

For now will I break his yoke from off thee, and will burst thy bonds in sunder. Nah 1:13

And it shall come to pass in the day that the LORD shall give thee rest from thy sorrow, and from thy fear, and from the hard bondage wherein thou wast made to serve,

That thou shalt take up this proverb against the king of Babylon, and say, How hath the oppressor ceased! the golden city ceased!

The LORD hath broken the staff of the wicked, [and] the sceptre of the rulers. Isa 14:3-5

Prayers

1. Oh Lord, arise and deliver me from all forms of failure in the name of Jesus.
2. Every stronghold of failure in my life and business be destroyed in the name of Jesus.
3. Every altar of failure erected against my life and business, be destroyed in the name of Jesus.
4. Every mark of failure, emblem of failure, identity of failure upon my life and business, be removed, erased and cease forever in the name of Jesus.
5. Every strongman of failure in my life die in the name of Jesus.
6. Every yoke of failure in my life, be destroyed by the blood of Jesus.
7. Arrows of failure fired into my life and business, I command you to come out and backfire in the name of Jesus.
8. Every instrument of failure erected against my life be destroyed in the name of Jesus.
9. Every captivity in my life, allowing repeated failure, be removed in the name of Jesus.
10. Every anointing of failure in my life, dry up in the name of Jesus.

11. Every ancestral curse of failure in my life be canceled in the name of Jesus.

12. Every hand of failure, holding me down to one spot, release me and wither in the name of Jesus.

13. Every garment of failure upon my life be removed and consumed by the fire of the Holy Ghost in the name of Jesus.

14. Any where I have been tied, oh Lord, go there and lose me in the name of Jesus.

15. Any room of failure I have been locked up, oh Lord open it and release me from that room in the name of Jesus.

16. Every valley of failure I have been kept, where my business has be tied, oh Lord by your power, release my business and release me from that valley in the name of Jesus.

17. Every blood of failure flowing in my veins, dry up by the authority in the name of Jesus.

18. Every shoe of failure on my feet be removed in the name of Jesus.

19. Every pollution in my life causing failure be neutralize by the blood of Jesus.

20. Every pollution in this business causing failure be neutralize in the name of Jesus.

21. Every seed of failure in my life be uprooted and destroyed in the name of Jesus.

22. Every pattern of failure program into my life, be reversed in the name of Jesus.

23. Every vehicle of failure in my life, catch fire in the name of Jesus.

24. Every name of failure given to me, I change it in the name of Jesus.

25. Every attack and effort of the enemy me to keep me in the captivity of failure, be destroyed in the name of Jesus.

26. Every witchcraft operation, marine operation, occultic operation, negative dream operation engineering repeated failure in my life, be destroyed by the authority in the name of Jesus.

27. Every ancestral power of failure holding me down, release me in the name of Jesus and go into captivity forever in the name of Jesus.

28. Anointing of success fall upon my life in the name of Jesus

29. Doors of success open unto me in the name of Jesus.

30. Every concluded work of the enemy to make me end a failure in life and business is aborted by fire in the name of Jesus.

31. Opportunity leading to success be made available for me in the name of Jesus.

32. Power to succeed in life and business possess me in the name of Jesus.

33. Any power that has vowed that I will not succeed, I break your vow and command your destruction in the name of Jesus.

34. Every door way of success that has been blocked against me, be opened in the name of Jesus.

35. Oh Lord, launch me into success in the name of Jesus.

36. Oh Lord, thank you for answered prayers.

CHAPTER 41

PRAYER FOR DIVINE SUPPLY

Samson then said, "With the jawbone of a donkey I have left them in heaps; with the jawbone of a donkey I have struck down a thousand men!" When he finished speaking, he threw the jawbone down and named that place Ramath Lehi. He was very thirsty, so he cried out to the LORD and said, "You have given your servant this great victory. But now must I die of thirst and fall into hands of the Philistines?" So God split open the basin at Lehi and water flowed out from it. When he took a drink, his strength was restored and he revived. For this reason he named the spring En Hakkore. It remains in Lehi to this very day. Judges 15:16-19 (Net Bible). Judge 15:16-19

God is a God of provision. He is the source of every good things. God wants to proof he is God in meeting the needs of men. Every business and business man needs divine supplies in other to run their business on profit and ease.

Divine supply is the art of God, the involvement of God in meeting all the needs of your organization in a supernatural way.

Areas Of Divine Supply
1. Human resources.
2. Idea supply.
3. Quality and quantity Customer supply.
4. Unimaginable business profit.
5. Financial supply.

God supplying the need of your organization does not make you to be lazy, it only makes your work to be productive. When you are working or planting, he his busy supplying all the needs of the organization. He can supply all your needs according to his riches in glory. Divine supply is not just God supplying your need, it is God making you a source of unending supply to others need. It will put an end to needs in your life and business forever.

Some Cases of divine supply

1. Now a wife of one of the prophets appealed to Elisha for help, saying, "Your servant, my husband is dead. You know that your servant was a loyal follower of the LORD. Now the creditor is coming to take away my two boys to be his servants." Elisha said to her, "What can I do for you? Tell me, what do you have in the house?" She answered, "Your servant has nothing in the house except a small jar of olive oil." He said, "Go and ask all your neighbors for empty containers. Get as many as you can. Go and close the door behind you and your sons. Pour the olive oil into all the containers; set aside each one when you have filled it." So she left him and closed the door behind her and her sons. As they were bringing the containers to her, she was pouring the olive oil. When the containers were full, she said to one of her sons, "Bring me another container." But he answered her, "There are no more." Then the olive oil stopped flowing. She went and told the prophet. He said, "Go, sell the olive oil. Repay your creditor, and then you and your sons can live off the rest of the profit." 2Kgs 4:1-7

2. And Jesus departed from thence, and came nigh unto the sea of Galilee; and went up into a mountain, and sat down there. And great multitudes came unto him, having with them [those that were] lame, blind, dumb,

183

maimed, and many others, and cast them down at Jesus' feet; and he healed them: Insomuch that the multitude wondered, when they saw the dumb to speak, the maimed to be whole, the lame to walk, and the blind to see: and they glorified the God of Israel. Then Jesus called his disciples [unto him], and said, I have compassion on the multitude, because they continue with me now three days, and have nothing to eat: and I will not send them away fasting, lest they faint in the way. And his disciples say unto him, Whence should we have so much bread in the wilderness, as to fill so great a multitude? And Jesus saith unto them, How many loaves have ye? And they said, Seven, and a few little fishes.

And he commanded the multitude to sit down on the ground. And he took the seven loaves and the fishes, and gave thanks, and brake [them], and gave to his disciples, and the disciples to the multitude. And they did all eat, and were filled: and they took up of the broken [meat] that was left seven baskets full. And they that did eat were four thousand men, beside women and children. And he sent away the multitude, and took ship, and came into the coasts of Magdala. Matt 15:29-39

Everyone is entitled to demand for their own supply because without demand from above there will be no supply.

Benefits Of Divine Supply
1. It makes you a source of blessing to your community.
2. It limits unnecessary and sometimes necessary expenses.
3. It makes you have more than enough to do business with.
4. It makes people delight in working with your organization
5. It makes your business a fruitful vine.
6. It enables easy spreading, enlargement and expansion.

7. It shut doors to loses completely and bring abundant gain.

Scriptural confession:

[When] the poor and needy seek water, and [there is] none, [and] their tongue faileth for thirst, I the LORD will hear them, I the God of Israel will not forsake them. I will open rivers in high places, and fountains in the midst of the valleys: I will make the wilderness a pool of water, and the dry land springs of water. Isa 41:17-18

Thou openest thine hand, and satisfiest the desire of every living thing. Ps 145:16

Prayers

1. Channels of divine supply from God to me, open in the name of Jesus.
2. Oh Lord, release the anointing of divine supply over my head in the name of Jesus.
3. Oh Lord, release the angels of divine supply into this organization.
4. Doors of divine supply, open in the name of Jesus.

CHAPTER 42

VICTORY OVER NEGATIVE DREAM

For God speaketh once, yea twice, [yet man] perceiveth it not. In a dream, in a vision of the night, when deep sleep falleth upon men, in slumberings upon the bed; Then he openeth the ears of men, and sealeth their instruction, That he may withdraw man [from his] purpose, and hide pride from man.
He keepeth back his soul from the pit, and his life from perishing by the sword. Job 33:14-18

Dream gift is implanted in men by God. Dream is a vehicle through which God communicate to man in words and pictures. God uses the channel of dream to give you direction, ideas, information leading to revelation. Whatever revelation God shows you through dream is to solve your problem.

However the devil too uses dream as a medium of perpetuating his evil operation. The devil uses dream as a medium of sowing evil seeds, manipulation, set back and failure.

But while men slept, his enemy came and sowed tares among the wheat, and went his way. Matt 13:25

The operation of the enemy is to sow bad dream. Negative dreams have the power to corrupt life negatively. Through dream the devil can dismantle lives and business. It is one of the best platforms the devil use in introducing problems and failure into people's lives.

The good news is that God is the custodian of dream, and He is alive to reverse and destroy all the works done into your business and life through evil dream.

Scriptural confession:

I will overturn, overturn, overturn, it: and it shall be no [more], until he come whose right it is; and I will give it [him]. Ezek 21:27

To turn aside the right of a man before the face of the most High, To subvert a man in his cause, the Lord approveth not. Who [is] he [that] saith, and it cometh to pass, [when] the Lord commandeth [it] not? Lam 3:35-37

But he answered and said, Every plant, which my heavenly Father hath not planted, shall be rooted up. Matt 15:13

And the Lord shall deliver me from every evil work, and will preserve [me] unto his heavenly kingdom: to whom [be] glory forever and ever. Amen. 2Tim 4:18

Prayers
1. Blood of Jesus flow into my life, erase every program of evil dreams in the name of Jesus.
2. Every dream battles in my life, be destroyed in the name of Jesus.

3. Every power manifesting negatively against my life through dream, be arrested by the authority in the name of Jesus.

4. Every covenant binding me to the power of negative dream, be broken in the name of Jesus.

5. I release myself from every covenant of negative dream in Jesus name.

6. Any power that has made my dream a platform for evil operation and battle against my life, be destroyed by the fire of the Holy Ghost in the name of Jesus.

7. Every dream that has been programmed to repeat itself in my life at certain season of my life, I command you to be aborted by fire in the name of Jesus.

8. Anointing of freedom from negative dream, come upon my life in Jesus name.

9. Oh Lord, deliver me permanently from the stronghold of negative dreams in the name of Jesus.

10. Oh Lord, set up a divine dream monitor in my life in the name of Jesus.

11. Thank you Lord for answered prayers.

CHAPTER 43

PRAYER FOR UNCOMMON BUSINESS BREAKTHROUGH

For by thee I have run through a troop; and by my God have I leaped over a wall. Ps 18:29

Every business needs a breakthrough. The word breakthrough, means to break a barrier of limitation through to platform of success. Break through simply means to break something through. If a door key is missing and your treasures are behind the door, it takes force to kick the door and get it opened. It takes determination like that to break something through.

See a picture of breakthrough in Peter's case:
Now when he had left speaking, he said unto Simon, Launch out into the deep, and let down your nets for a draught. And Simon answering said unto him, Master, we have toiled all the night, and have taken nothing: nevertheless at thy word I will let down the net. And when they had this done, they inclosed a great multitude of fishes: and their net brake. Luke 5:7 And they beckoned unto [their] partners, which were in the other ship, that they should come and help them. And they came, and filled both the ships, so that they began to sink. Luke 5:4-7

Jesus created a platform of breakthrough for Peter, the kind of fish he has not caught before, he caught in few hours. That is breakthrough. Breakthrough is a business profit margin and sales experience that will surpass your plans.

Breakthrough is like the total sum of what should happen in ten years put together to happen in one day.

Breakthrough is an overnight success beyond your dream, engineer by divine intervention that you cannot explain. Often time, breakthrough is not what you can explain.

Benefit of breakthrough
1. It brings divine shift.
2. It brings instant recognition.
3. It draws attention to your organization.
4. It takes you far beyond your plans.
5. It changes your business level.
6. It put your business in a new light and platform.

Scriptural confession
I can do all things through Christ which strengthened me. Phil 4:13
Nay, in all these things we are more than conquerors through him that loved us. Rom 8:37
Ye are of God, little children, and have overcome them: because greater is he that is in you, than he that is in the world. 1John 4:4.
Ask of me, and I shall give [thee] the heathen [for] thine inheritance, and the uttermost parts of the earth [for] thy possession. Ps 2:8

Prayer
1. Oh Lord, give me a breakthrough in business in Jesus name.

2. Doors of mega breakthrough, open unto me in Jesus name.

3. Event that will bring about breakthrough in my life, oh Lord cause it to happen in Jesus name.

4. Every obstacle to my breakthrough be removed by fire in the name of Jesus.

5. I activate my business breakthrough miracle in the name of Jesus.

6. Oh Ye heavens of my breakthrough open by fire in the name of Jesus.

7. Every anti breakthrough forces and programs against my life and business, be arrested and subdued in the name of Jesus.

44

PRAYING FOR THE ECONOMY OF THE STATE OF YOUR BUSINESS OPERATION

Pray for the peace of Jerusalem: they shall prosper that love thee. Peace be within thy walls, [and] prosperity within thy palaces. Ps 122:6-7

God has control over every situation. If the economy of your country of operation is bad, it will likely affect your business. Over inflation will affect the sales of goods, it will affect the price of goods and services. When the cost of raw material is higher than the cost of the product sales will be slow.

God is interested in the economy of every nation. He owns every nation.

The earth [is] the LORD'S, and the fulness thereof; the world, and they that dwell therein. Ps 24:1

God has not removed his hands from the affairs of men. He rules and reigns over the affairs of men. He is called the governor among the nation. Ps. 22:28.

Through your consistent prayer over the business and economy, God will make your business to thrive in the bad economy and makes the economy favor you while is biting others.

When [men] are cast down, then thou shalt say, [There is] lifting up; and
he shall save the humble person. Job 22:29

When God turn things in your business favor, then when others are saying there is a casting down, it will be a lifting up for your business.

For I know the thoughts that I think toward you, saith the LORD,
thoughts of peace, and not of evil, to give you an expected end. Jer 29:11

God wants the best for you. The plan of God for you is a plan of success in business and in life.

Many companies often close down in bad economic crunch because they don't look up to the face of God for divine intervention. When there was famine in Egypt, God led Isaac to do his business and God caused him to reap hundred fold returns in the midst of the famine. *Gen. 26:1-12*. God is able to do exceedingly abundantly above what you ask or think according to the power that works in you. *Eph. 3:20*.

There are two kinds of Economy
1. Man's economy:
Man's economy is a natural economy that work based on certain laws of supply and demand, invest and harvest etc. The economy of man works on facts. Whatever goes up must come down. The facts are what we see. The economy of man is however subject to inflation, rise and fall in the market, it is subject to crash and crunch. The

economy is not perfectly predictable, as anything can happen to it anytime.

2. **Divine economy:**

Divine economy is the economy of God in the midst of his children. Divine economy is not subject to the laws of nature, but the laws of the kingdom. It does not work on facts and figures but on faith and instructions. However, this same economy is operated here on earth and not in heaven. Jesus defies all economic law when he turns five loaves and two fishes to plenty to feed over five thousand men, excluding women and children. While he fed women and children from it, and 12 basket was still left over.

And they say unto him, We have here but five loaves, and two fishes. He said, Bring them hither to me. And he commanded the multitude to sit down on the grass, and took the five loaves, and the two fishes, and looking up to heaven, he blessed, and brake, and gave the loaves to [his] disciples, and the disciples to the multitude. And they did all eat, and were filled: and they took up of the fragments that remained twelve baskets full. And they that had eaten were about five thousand men, beside women and children. Matt 14:17-21

This violated all economic laws, facts and figures. It happened here on earth, and not in heaven.

This same God is still ruling over the affairs of men. He performed such operation easily. In 2kings 7:1-2 , similar occurrence happens, God overturned over inflation and famine and dropped the prices of every goods from highest cost to lowest cost, that the poorest among the poor could afford to buy what he needs for his survival, all within 24hours.

When God steps into the economy of a country, he overturns it from natural economic operation to divine economic operation. He will remove every law, facts and figures, and make the economy favor all and balance it. The truth is that God wants to do that all the time.

Trust in God for intervention over the economy and he will bring in his own divine plan to stabilize the economy in your business favor.

Scriptural confession
Read Isaiah 60, and the following.
Now unto him that is able to do exceeding abundantly above all that we ask or think, according to the power that worketh in us, Eph 3:20
When [men] are cast down, then thou shalt say, [There is] lifting up; and he shall save the humble person. Job 22:29

Prayers
1. Any power that wants to shut down the economy of this city, I bind you and cast you out in the name of Jesus.
2. Every stronghold of darkness, to crush the economy of this city, be pulled down in the name of Jesus.
3. Every wind and storm of economic failure, I command you in the name of Jesus, disappear forever.
4. Any marine power, territorial power, prince of darkness ruling over the economy of this city, be arrested by the thunder and fire of God in the name of Jesus.

5. Every concluded works of darkness to crash this city's economy be averted and aborted in the name of Jesus.

6. Every economic failure be reversed in the mighty name of Jesus.

7. Every evil economic failure supervisor be arrested by fire in the name of Jesus.

8. I command stability in the economy of this state in the name of Jesus.

9. Oh Lord, intervene in the economy of this state in the name of Jesus.

10. Every wrong business and economic decisions taken by the government that can affect the economy of this city negatively, oh Lord overturn it in the name of Jesus.

11. Any crisis' that can happen and affect our business and economy let it be stopped in the name of Jesus.

CHAPTER 45

PRAYER AGAINST WITCHCRAFT ATTACKS

And I will cut off witchcrafts out of thine hand; and thou shalt have no [more] soothsayers: Mic. 5:12

God is against witchcraft and He is willing to deliver you from the oppression and operation of this demonic spirits. The operation of witchcraft has brought many potentially gifted people to an hopeless being. Witchcraft operation is the activities of wicked agent of darkness, on evil errand to oppress, manipulate, afflict and destroy people's destiny. Witchcraft operation is rampart everywhere. Many are under the oppression of witchcraft attacks and operation.

Witchcraft is a major tool in the hand of the devil with the vast network in virtually every streets, family, schools, institution, organizations and society. Witchcraft is a serious satanic activity to shortchange, to steal, to kill, to destroy good things. It is the act of deception, wickedness and display of supernatural power to subject their victim to punishment, suffering and difficulties in every area. Witchcraft activity cannot be undermined; it has to be addressed through the power of God and fervent prayer to cut off her evil operation.

Weapons of witchcraft operation
1. Curses, spell and evil oaths.

2. Manipulation and oppression.
3. Exchanging of glory, destinies and virtues.
4. Mind blackness, confusion.
5. Spiritual remote control.
6. Donation of human lives, souls and body parts.
7. Perversion and affliction.
8. Evil judgment.
9. Poverty and lack.
10. Merciless attacks leading to great loses and destruction.
11. Evil setup and unjust punishment.

Symptoms of witchcraft attacks

1. Stubborn and repeated problem.
2. Repeated attacks and frustration.
3. Unexplainable hindrance and difficulties.
4. Abnormal behavioral patterns and wrong actions.
5. Unusual hatred.
6. Unusual delay and failure.
7. Chain like bondage and stagnation.
8. Perversion and addiction.
9. Strange health cases.
10. Sudden downfall and debt.
11. Unexplainable crisis and disaster.
12. Mind control and manipulation
13. Aborted plans.
14. Cobwebs, blockages and mysterious appearances of it.
15. Failure at the edge of breakthrough.
16. Unexplainable disappointment.
17. Unexplainable attack.
18. Demonic dreams and negative manifestation.
19. Constant and repeated accident.

20. Strange animal attacks and monitoring.

21. Joblessness, helplessness and hopelessness.

22. Death and evil occurrence.

23. Seeing evil things.

24. Addiction to smoking, alcohol and immoralities.

25. Hearing strange voices and instruction.

26. Abnormal terminal diseases.

27. Eating food in the dreams.

28. Having sex in the dream to abort good things. etc

How to overcome

1. Give your life to Jesus.
2. Go for deliverance.
3. Have faith in God.
4. Embark on several days of fasting and prayers of deliverance.
5. Draw close to God.

Scriptural confession

And the Lord shall deliver me from every evil work, and will preserve [me] unto his heavenly kingdom: to whom [be] glory for ever and ever. Amen. 2Tim 4:18

Thou shalt not suffer a witch to live. Exod 22:18

And ye shall know the truth, and the truth shall make you free. John 8:32

If the Son therefore shall make you free, ye shall be free indeed. John 8:36.

Further read Psalm 27, Ps. 35

Prayers

1. Oh Lord intervene in my case and deliver me from all witchcraft attacks and operation in the name of Jesus

2. Every witchcraft operation against my destiny, die in the name of Jesus.

3. Every witchcraft curse and decrees against me be cancelled in the name of Jesus.

4. Every witchcraft weapons fashioned against me, catch-fire in Jesus name.

5. Every witchcraft agents attacking my life, release me and die in Jesus name.

6. Every witchcraft works prepared and done against my life die in the name of Jesus.

7. All witchcrafts obstacles and hindrances on my way be removed in the name of Jesus.

8. Every witchcraft bondage in my life be destroyed in the name of Jesus.

9. Every witchcraft assignments over my life be terminated in the name of Jesus.

10. Any witchcraft arrow in my life, backfire in the name of Jesus.

11. Every witchcraft seed and plantation in my life, be uprooted in the name of Jesus.

12. Any witchcraft power holding and diverting my blessing release it and die in the name of Jesus.

13. Every witchcraft chain holding me down, break by the authority in the name of Jesus.

14. Every throne of witchcraft in my life, catch-fire in the name of Jesus.

15. Every witchcraft oath and covenant holding me down, break in the name of Jesus.

16. Every limitation placed upon my life by witchcraft agents be removed in the name of Jesus.

17. Deliverance fire of God set me free from all witchcraft installation, manifestation and oppression in the name of Jesus.
18. Consuming fire of God, consume every network of witches in my life in the name of Jesus.
19. Son of God set me free from witchcraft and their operation in the name of Jesus.
20. Every of my lost years as a result of witchcraft operation, be restored in the name of Jesus.
21. Thank you Lord for answered prayers.

CHAPTER 46

PERSONAL DELIVERANCE PRAYERS

Deliver thyself as a roe from the hand [of the hunter], and as a bird from the hand of the fowler. Prov. 6:5

Personal deliverance is necessary for freedom and progress. Any man under bondage and captivity of any kind needs deliverance. Deliverance starts from knowing the truth. The truth is the deliverer himself.

It is not only knowing the truth that sets you free, but applying the truth that you know to your situation. That is the purpose of personal deliverance prayers. God is willing to deliver you if you are willing to be free.

Deliver thyself, O Zion, that dwellest [with] the daughter of Babylon. Zech 2:7

All things have been settled concerning your deliverance from the hands of the enemy. Personal deliverance prayers are a prayer that teaches you how to undergo personal deliverance from bondage, challenges, sins, etc through the leading of the Holy Spirit.

Deliverance means to be set free from bondage, captivity, attacks, sickness, infirmity and any evil thing God's has not planted in your life. To be liberated from oppression, destruction, infection and anything that is making life a living hell for you. The word of God is the deliverance force of God. He sent his word and it heals and delivers them from their destruction. God has given you the weapon of deliverance which is his word, and you are been challenged to make your deliverance a reality.

Keys To Deliverance

1. Willingness:

For if there be first a willing mind, [it is] accepted according to that a man hath, [and] not according to that he hath not. 2Cor 8:12.

It takes willingness to obey any given instruction. Your willingness is the first key. A willing mind is a made up mind. Freedom is easy when your mind is made up. You will easily receive divine backing of God to be delivered.

2. Faith:

But without faith [it is] impossible to please [him]: for he that cometh to God must believe that he is, and [that] he is a rewarder of them that diligently seek him. Heb 11:6

Faith believes in all the written and spoken word of God to be yea and amen. Your faith reflects your boldness in the work of the Lord Jesus, wherefore it says, whom the son of man has set free is free indeed.

3. Prayer:

And call upon me in the day of trouble: I will deliver thee, and thou shalt glorify me. Ps 50:15.

Prayer is a key weapon in deliverance from all oppression. It takes prayer to confront your adversary and with faith you conquer.

Areas of deliverance

1. Mind deliverance.
2. Financial deliverance.
3. Health deliverance.
4. Business deliverance.
5. Products deliverance.
6. Business ground deliverance.
7. Equipment and tools deliverance.
8. Your business team deliverance.

How to Start Deliverance Process

1. Accept Jesus into your life now:

   Declare this: Lord Jesus, come into my life, and save me. Forgive all my sins and have mercy on me. I accept you as my personal Lord and Saviour. Write my names in the book of Life and hear my voice anytime and I call on your name in Jesus name.
2. Ask for the mercy of God
3. Ask for the Spirit of God into your life
4. Pray as instructed

Scriptures for deliverance

Read out these scriptures into anointing oil
Luke 10:19, 2Tim. 4:18, John 8:32, Rom. 16:20, 1John 4:4, 1John 3:8, Gal. 3:13-14, John 14:13-14.
Now the Lord is that Spirit: and where the Spirit of the Lord [is], there [is] liberty. 2Cor 3:17.

Prayers

1. I receive mercy in the name of Jesus.
2. I invite the Holy Spirit to come and help and deliver me in the name of Jesus.
3. Oh Lord my father, fill my mouth with fire in the name of Jesus.
4. Holy Ghost fire, fill my mouth in the name of Jesus.
5. I renounce every evil covenant in my life in the name of Jesus.
6. I renounce every agreement and connection binding me with any wrong and evil association physically and spiritually in the name of Jesus.
7. Any evil covenant binding me to battle, challenge and evil I command you to break in the name of Jesus.
8. I deliver myself from every evil altar in the name of Jesus.
9. I deliver my name from every altar in the name of Jesus.
10. I release fire of the Holy Spirit upon my spirit, and soul and body, and send out every stranger dwelling in any part of my body in Jesus name.
11. I enter into the covenant of the blood of Jesus and I break every old covenant disturbing my life in the name of Jesus.
12. Any curse working against my life and breakthrough, be cancelled by the blood of Jesus.
13. Every force maintaining curses in my life, I am no more a candidate of that curse, for Christ has redeemed me from the curse of the law and he has been made a curse for me, therefore there is no condemnation to those who walk in the spirit and not after the flesh, I command you to lose your old over my life in Jesus name.

14. Every weapon of darkness that is fashioned to keep my destiny in bondage be destroyed by the fire of the Holy Ghost in the name of Jesus.
15. Every mark of the enemy upon my life, I cancel you with the blood of Jesus in the name of Jesus.
16. Every ancestral power attached to the affairs of my life, release me and die in the name of Jesus.
17. Every familiar spirit assigned against my life, release me and die in the name of Jesus.
18. Shout it loud, Holy Ghost fire, set me free in Jesus name.
19. God of deliverance, send your word of deliverance into my life in the name of Jesus.
20. Every bondage in my life, I set you on fire in the name of Jesus.
21. I lose myself from all forms of bondage, chains and captivity in the mighty name of Jesus.
22. Oh Lord, change my story from henceforth in Jesus name.

CHAPTER 47

DEALING WITH NEGATIVE FORCES WITHIN

The stranger that [is] within thee shall get up above thee very high; and thou shalt come down very low. Deut. 28:43

There are forces that live within every man. It is either a force of push or force of setback. It is important a man identifies the kind of force that operates within him. The force that operates within you will determine how far you go in life. As you know, force is a repelling energy or a propelling energy. It either repels you from doing what will prosper your business or propels you. The operation of these forces determines the situation of things in your life.

More than one force can operate in your life. Negative force is a force that cause retardation and set back. These forces are programmed to debar progress and frustrate plans.

Some examples of this forces are listed below:
force of failure, force of discouragement, the force of fear, force of rising and falling, force of excuses, force of laziness, force of procrastination, force of confusion, force of shallow mindedness, force of manipulation.

It is crucial to know the kind of force that works within you that can be of a negative effect to your business and promptly deal with that force and send it out of you.

How to get rid of it
1. Locate the force.
2. Send it out.
3. Be filled with the spirit of God.

Scriptural confession
As soon as they hear of me, they shall obey me: the strangers shall submit themselves unto me.
The strangers shall fade away, and be afraid out of their close places. Ps 18:44-45
So shall ye know that I [am] the LORD your God dwelling in Zion, my holy mountain: then shall Jerusalem be holy, and there shall no strangers pass through her any more. Joel 3:17
But he answered and said, Every plant, which my heavenly Father hath not planted, shall be rooted up.
Matt 15:13

Prayers
1. Oh Lord, deliver me from every negative force in my life.
2. Any force of failure in my life, I send you out by the authority in the name of Jesus.
3. Every force of rejection in my life, I cast you out by the authority in the name of Jesus.
4. Every force of manipulation, stagnation and reproach, I cast you out in the name of Jesus.

5. I disband and stop every operation of negative forces in the name of Jesus.

6. I command total evacuation of every anti progress forces in my life in Jesus name.

7. Every force of excuse, I send you out in Jesus name.

8. Every force of fear, I send you out in the name of Jesus.

9. I command the force of light to possess me in the name of Jesus.

10. Every habitation of stranger in me, be destroyed by fire in the name of Jesus.

11. I pull down every habitation of strangers in Jesus name.

12. I release myself from the hold of every negative force in Jesus name.

13. I command the force of light to enter me in the name of Jesus.

14. Thank you Lord for answered prayers.

CHAPTER 48

BREAKING THE YOKE
AND SPELL OF POVERTY

And it shall come to pass in that day, [that] his burden shall be taken away from off thy shoulder, and his yoke from off thy neck, and the yoke shall be destroyed because of the anointing. Isa 10:27

The focus of this book is actually to help you pray your business to a level of breakthrough. If there is a yoke upon the business owner, the yoke will affect the business breakthrough.

A yoke is a kind of bondage that ties someone to something. When a yoke is tying a man to poverty, that means the man is under the spell of poverty. In order word, it means such a man can never succeed with any business idea in his hand. No matter the level of business idea he has, it will end in failure. The force of poverty is a force that keeps his victim in the valley of reproach and lack. It diverts away provisions and needed resources from such a person, so it is not something that must be taken likely.

As a business that wants to succeed, you must take into consideration that a grace of prosperity upon a business man will propel the business into prosperity. There is no business without the pioneer behind it. *The destiny of the business is connected to the destiny of the owner.* If the owner is under a spell, then the business will be under a spell. Business is a delicate entity. If money is a taboo in the hand of the business owner that means money will be a taboo in the business.

Breaking the yoke of poverty ensures that you are personally free from the bondage of poverty and launched into the life of freedom to make money as much as you want. If the yoke is upon you, money will be far from you. In order word, the more you strive to have it, the more it will be impossible to get it. It is only when the yokes are broken that the access to financial fortune will be available. That is the reason you must deal with this with deep understanding and pray every prayer with obedient to the instruction.

Keys to freedom
1. Get anointing oil and pray into it.
2. Embark on 3 days fasting and prayer.
3. Pray the prayers in this book and close your prayers each day by anointing yourself and proclaiming blessing upon yourself and the business you are doing.

Scriptural confession:
And it shall come to pass in that day, [that] his burden shall be taken away from off thy shoulder, and his yoke from off thy neck, and the yoke shall be destroyed because of the anointing. Isa 10:27

For now will I break his yoke from off thee, and will burst thy bonds in sunder. Nah 1:13

Prayers

1. Every spell of poverty in my life be destroyed in the name of Jesus.

2. Any yoke of poverty in my life, be removed and destroyed in the name of Jesus.

3. Every mark of limitation to poverty and failure in me be cancelled and destroyed in Jesus name.

4. Every active bondage of poverty in my life be destroyed in Jesus name.

5. I reject poverty in Jesus name, every curse of poverty operating in my life be cancelled in the name of Jesus.

6. I redeem myself with the blood of Jesus from every curse and bondage of poverty in Jesus name.

7. Every demonic forces at work to keep me in the bondage of poverty, I am not your candidate, release me by fire in the name of Jesus.

8. Every evil pattern of lack and poverty in my life and family, be destroyed by the blood of Jesus.

9. Every assignment of ancestral powers over my life, be terminated in the name of Jesus.

10. Every network of poverty in my life, break into pieces in the name of Jesus.

11. Every curse of poverty operating in my life and family be canceled by the blood of Jesus in the name of Jesus.

12. Anointing of prosperity, my life is available, possess me in the name of Jesus Christ.

13. I command total restoration of all my virtue and blessings in the name of Jesus.

14. Anything assigned to swallow my blessings and riches, vomit it and catch fire in Jesus name.

15. Mantle of riches fall upon me in the name of Jesus Christ.

CHAPTER 49

HOLY SPIRIT, YOUR BUSINESS PARTNER

Then he answered and spake unto me, saying, This [is] the word of the LORD unto Zerubbabel, saying, Not by might, nor by power, but by my spirit, saith the LORD of hosts. Zech 4:6

Holy Spirit is the spirit of God. Holy Spirit is a compulsory spirit for all believers; He is the promise of God to all the children of God. The presence of Holy Spirit in you is simply the presence of God in you. When the Holy Spirit operates as your partner in business, the business will experience only supernatural breakthrough. Every event that will be happening around the business will be supernatural, because everything about the Holy Spirit is special. There is nothing natural about him.

Making Holy Spirit your business partner will make your business to scale all height, and succeed beyond the input of man. Holy Spirit is a living force; it is a Spirit that can do all things.

When God was creating the earth, Holy spirit was at work to perform everything God said.

Gen 1:2 And the earth was without form, and void; and darkness [was] upon the face of the deep. And the Spirit of God moved upon the face of the waters.

The earth has no form, but the Spirit gives it form as God speaks. Whatever God says, God saw because Holy Spirit makes a thing real.

And God said, Let there be light: and there was light. Gen 1:3

God did nothing without the Spirit. The Spirit makes all things work and makes nothing wastes. There is nothing that is hidden from him and there is nothing that is impossible with Him. The presence of the Holy Spirit in your business is the beginning of progress.

The Operations Of The Holy Spirit

- He is a revealer. 1Cor. 2:9-12
  He reveals deep secret that no one knows.
- He is an instructor. Ps.32:8
  He instruct believer in what to do to make headway.
- He is a deliverer. 2Cor. 3:17
  He helps a believer to be delivered from bondage.
- He is a teacher. 1Cor.2:13
  He teach believer the word of God and give them deep understanding of it.
- He is an intercessor. Rom. 8:26
  He prays on your behalf and helps your infirmity.
- He is a comforter. John 16:7
  He gives word of encouragement that brings healing in time of worries.
- He is a helper. Rom. 8:26
  He send help your way when you are stranded.

- He is director. Isaiah 30:21

  He orders your step in the way you should take.

- He is a strengthener. Rom. 8:11

  He gives you strength when you are weak and divine ability to do more than the ordinary human power.

- He is a performer. Gen. 1:2-3

  He carries out your plans and dreams and make it a reality.

- He is a counselor. Isaiah 11:2

  He gives the best advice to those who put their trust in Him. Since Holy Spirit is also God, He knows everything and has the solution to every problem.

How to get the Spirit involved

1. Be filled with the Spirit
2. Obey the voice of the Spirit.

Scriptural confession

And it shall come to pass afterward, [that] I will pour out my spirit upon all flesh; and your sons and your daughters shall prophesy, your old men shall dream dreams, your young men shall see visions: Joel 2:28

And it shall come to pass in the last days, saith God, I will pour out of my Spirit upon all flesh: and your sons and your daughters shall prophesy, and your young men shall see visions, and your old men shall dream dreams: Acts 2:17

If ye then, being evil, know how to give good gifts unto your children: how much more shall [your] heavenly Father give the Holy Spirit to them that ask him? Luke 11:13

Prayers

1. Oh Lord, fill me with your spirit in Jesus name.
2. Anointing of the Holy Spirit possess me in Jesus name.
3. Holy Spirit, I am ready take my temple in Jesus name.